THE UNTHINKABLE SACRIFICE

KALOS

The word *kalos* (καλός) means beautiful. It is the call of the good; that which arouses interest, desire: "I am here." Beauty brings the appetite to rest at the same time as it wakens the mind from its daily slumber, calling us to look afresh at that which is before our very eyes. It makes virgins of us all, and of everything—there, before us, lies something that we never noticed before. Beauty consists in *integritas sive perfectio* (integrity and perfection) and *claritas* (brightness/clarity). It is the reason why we rise and why we sleep—that great night of dependence, one that reveals the borrowed existence of all things, if, that is, there is to be a thing at all, or if there is to be a person at all. Here lies the ground of all science, of philosophy, and of all theology, indeed, of our each and every day.

This series will seek to provide intelligent-yet-accessible volumes that have the innocence of beauty and of true adventure, and in so doing remind us all again of that which we took for granted, most of all thought itself.

SERIES EDITORS:
Conor Cunningham, and Joseph Terry

"'We were all children before being men.' This formula of Descartes finds its most perfect expression in the work of Zechariah Mickel. Childhood refers to parenthood, and parenthood to a particular form of love. With all the resources of phenomenology, the unthinkable sacrifice of Isaac here takes on meaning for each of us. Like Abraham on the day of Isaac's sacrifice, the child's face definitively deprives us of our pretensions to wanting to control everything. This book is a learning experience, and also a lesson. Because anyone who has exercised parenthood knows that there is sacrifice there, too. Because it is not enough to give. You still have to give yourself."

—EMMANUEL FALQUE, author of *The Metamorphosis of Finitude: An Essay on Birth and Resurrection*

"If phenomenology's promise to describe our experience can be hindered by the abstract nature of its concepts, Mickel's vivid and accessible prose provides readers a valuable entry point to the discussion. The meditation found in these pages seamlessly draws on key insights from contemporary French phenomenology to bring an experience philosophy has too rarely brought to explicit focus: the beautiful and terrible vulnerability of parenthood, and the joys of the sacrifice that this responsibility demands."

—STEPHANIE RUMPZA, author of *Phenomenology of the Icon: Mediating God Through the Image*

"Striking in its philosophical depth and poignant in its portrayal of human existence, Mickel's *The Unthinkable Sacrifice* is a wonder. As both a philosopher and a father, I found myself profoundly moved by Mickel's insights and reflections. A must-read for anyone seeking to comprehend the beautiful and tumultuous journey of fatherhood. I am glad to see that philosophers are still able to write such books."

—MARTIN KOCI, author of *Christianity After Christendom: Heretical Perspectives in Philosophical Theology*

"When my son was about six, he told me that he didn't want to be a philosopher because they don't spend time with their kids. Sadly, being good at philosophy doesn't automatically translate into being a good father. In an absolutely stunning work of subtle beauty and vulnerably concise argument, Zechariah Mickel offers a constructive phenomenological vision of fatherhood that simultaneously gives me hope and reassurance. I needed to read this book and so do you."

—J. AARON SIMMONS, author of *Camping with Kierkegaard*

"I don't know whether there are many things as philosophically and existentially massive as begetting and caring for a child, and the love that a man has for his own child is beyond comparison. Zechariah Mickel has written beautifully and lucidly about the joys and anguish of fatherhood. His words spring forth from his particular experiences, but these are essentially human. They will resonate deeply with anyone who has started upon the same path."

—STEVEN NEMES, author of *Theology of the Manifest: Christianity Without Metaphysics*

"Phenomenology is, first and foremost, about bringing us back to experience, back to the everydayness of life itself. What could be more pertinent, then, than a phenomenological examination of one of the most common (and yet, in contemporary society, neglected and devalued) experiences: parenting? In *The Unthinkable Sacrifice*, Mickel approaches this oft-overlooked topic with the attention and insight it demands. As a father who happens also to be a philosopher, I highly recommend this book."

—MATTHEW CLEMENTE, author of *Eros Crucified: Death, Desire, and the Divine in Psychoanalysis and Philosophy of Religion*

The Unthinkable Sacrifice

AN ESSAY ON FATHERHOOD

. . .

Zechariah Mickel

Foreword by Steven DeLay

CASCADE *Books* · Eugene, Oregon

THE UNTHINKABLE SACRIFICE
An Essay on Fatherhood

Cascade Books
An Imprint of Wipf and Stock Publishers
199 W. 8th Ave., Suite 3
Eugene, OR 97401

www.wipfandstock.com

PAPERBACK ISBN: 979-8-3852-1907-0
HARDCOVER ISBN: 979-8-3852-1908-7
EBOOK ISBN: 979-8-3852-1909-4

Cataloguing-in-Publication data:

Names: Mickel, Zechariah [author]. | DeLay, Steven [foreword writer].

Title: The unthinkable sacrifice : an essay on fatherhood / Zechariah Mickel.

Description: Eugene, OR: Cascade Books, 2025 | Series: Kalos series | Includes bibliographical references and index.

Identifiers: ISBN 979-8-3852-1907-0 (paperback) | ISBN 979-8-3852-1908-7 (hardcover) | ISBN 979-8-3852-1909-4 (ebook)

Subjects: LCSH: Fatherhood—Philosophy. | Phenomenology. | Child rearing—Philosophy. | Parent and child—Philosophy. | Parenting. | Parent–Child relations. | Child. | Parenthood—moral and ethical aspects. | Father-Child relations.

Classification: HQ769 M53 2025 (paperback) | HQ769 (ebook)

VERSION NUMBER 07/18/25

Earlier versions of chapters 1–3 were previously published with *GCAS Review*: "Caring for the Child's Soul in the Late Modern Maelstrom." *GCAS Review* 1.1 (2024). https://www.gcasreview.com/publications-religion-and-society. Reprinted (with significant revisions) with permission.

Scripture quotations are from The ESV® Bible (The Holy Bible, English Standard Version®), © 2001 by Crossway, a publishing ministry of Good News Publishers. Used by permission. All rights reserved.

A big thank you also to Ivanka Demchuk for permission to use her painting, "Hidden life in Nazareth," for the book's cover art.

For Poppy and Eloise.

Contents

Foreword

THERE IS AN OLD, familiar pedagogical saying that it is the teacher who by teaching learns more than the student. That truism is one held in particularly high regard in academic philosophical circles, owing to its supposed Socratic pedigree. Zechariah Mickel, to be sure, is a student of mine, insofar as he did an independent reading on French phenomenology for which I served as the instructor. But did I in any real sense teach him phenomenology? Truth be told, I think not. The truth of the matter, it seems to me, is that I almost certainly learned more from him during our experience of reading through Jean-Louis Chrétien, Michel Henry, Jean-Yves Lacoste, Jean-Luc Marion, Paul Ricœur, and Claude Romano together than he did from me. I do not say this as a rhetorical maneuver designed to allow me to invoke the adage about teaching. I say so, rather, because the text here that you are about to read from Mickel is a work of phenomenology (the work's chosen self-description, "Essay," is a subtle tip of the hat to what its author has learned and appropriated from Levinas's *Totality and Infinity*) that has taught me much I did not yet already know. It would be highly misleading, then, to suggest that *The Unthinkable Sacrifice: An Essay on Fatherhood* is in any important respect the result of its author's having studied with me. Nor, for that matter, is it a work purely reducible to the influence of the many phenomenological figures whom its author has read carefully. For as anyone who goes on to read the text for himself will recognize immediately, its author is someone who possesses a keen and distinctive phenomenological vision all his own. And quite frankly, that is something that simply cannot be taught.

Nevertheless, even a work of philosophy as original as this one invariably orients itself within an intellectual tradition of some kind. In this case, Mickel's essay openly and conscientiously situates itself within the phenomenological tradition of philosophy. In what way, exactly, is the work in question phenomenological? That question, of course, only raises the longstanding one regarding what phenomenology itself is. Mickel, who knows the relevant history, is not at all unaware of that question's importance. Since its inception with Husserl, the very idea of phenomenology has been a point of contestation among those who claim to be its practitioners. For that reason, it was Ricœur who insightfully, if provocatively, characterized the French reception of phenomenology as a series of "Husserlian heresies." And yet, its internal divisions and disagreements notwithstanding, the history of phenomenology is not ultimately just a story of patricide. Yes, the record undeniably shows that Husserl is often challenged, and in some respects his views are frequently rejected, by his own philosophical descendants (many of whom in the early stages of phenomenology were at one point his personal students or protégés), yet there always remains an unmistakable family resemblance nonetheless. Without notable exception, there are key agreements among its practitioners over phenomenology's method and matter. To begin with, the scientific reductionism and naturalism so common to other philosophical schools are dismissed in the name of a searching focus on the world as we perceive and experience it, whether that is said to be the lifeworld (Husserl), average everydayness (Heidegger), the perceived world (Merleau-Ponty), or so forth. In each case, the aim is to reveal the real, which is held to be a matter of the manifest, the given. Consequently, this entails that phenomenology as a philosophical approach proceeds by way of description, rather than by theoretical construction, metaphysical speculation, or rationalistic deduction. The task is to uncover and show a phenomenon, whatever it may be, rather than to argue for it. The end result of a successful phenomenological account, thus, is not a conclusion that one has been forced to accept through rational deduction, but instead an insight, a seeing, of what has been brought clearly into relief. Such is the approach Mickel himself will employ in the work here when casting his gaze on the phenomenon that interests him—namely, the phenomenon of fatherhood, or more precisely, the relation of love between father and child in all of its various dimensions, but above all, in light of the ethical call of responsibility the father experiences in the face of the child's vulnerability and dependence. In a fashion deliberately reminiscent of Levinas's "Face" or Chrétien's call and response, Mickel will characterize the father's identity—his very self as father—as arriving from an *elsewhere*, a phenomenon that in turn accordingly proves to be an instance of what Marion would term *revelation*, or Romano the *event*, inasmuch as to be oneself is to find oneself encountered by another who summons a response that has called one into question. To return to Ricœur, the phenomenon of fatherhood, as Mickel understands it, is a matter of finding "oneself as another," for being oneself in this case demands the sacrifice of one's own self for the sake of the other. The fulfillment of parental love, much like the *agape* upon which Mickel clearly intends us to see it modeled, requires self-abnegation.

Those who know the history of phenomenology just recounted will know why, then, it would only be both natural and tempting to further classify Mickel's work as a contribution to recent French phenomenology. The essay's terminology and style are clearly indebted to a number of the French figures cited previously. Yet it is a credit to Mickel's work that it defies any such banal ascription. For one thing, the very notion of there being such a thing as French phenomenology is very often misleading, and would be here—there is phenomenology that has been done in France, certainly, but what makes it distinctively French? Too often, the adjective is used as an excuse for ignorance—the implication is that it is phenomenology, and thus irrelevant to those who do analytic philosophy, and French, and so further irrelevant to those in the Anglophone world who work in Husserl or Heidegger studies. However, the truth is that there is nothing philosophically illuminating about the supposed distinction between "continental" and "analytic" philosophy. And in any case, Michel Henry was right when he said that for the twentieth century, phenomenology *is* philosophy. Many other philosophical movements, both analytic and continental, have long ago come and gone—yet phenomenology continues. It is not merely a historical movement, but a living philosophy. This is especially the case in Mickel's America, where Kevin Hart, Richard Kearney, and Anthony Steinbock, among others, have extended the work of the "theological turn" initiated in France. More recently, Brian Becker, Matthew Clemente, Adam J. Graves, Steven Nemes, as well as Joseph Rivera, Stephanie Rumpza, and J. Aaron Simmons, have contributed to this American reception of French phenomenology. Like the work by those just mentioned, Mickel's *The Unthinkable Sacrifice* is not an exercise in mere exegesis. It learns what is necessary from texts, and then in turn points us back to the things themselves. The reader, consequently, is sure to find the work's pages replete with subtle allusions to other phenomenological figures and texts. Mickel borrows liberally and judiciously from the phenomenologists with whom he is in conversation, particularly Marion and Levinas, but it is always done with an unwavering eye on what the description seeks to bring into view of the phenomenon, and has not yet otherwise been so.

A specific example will suffice to make the point. Marion has said that the philosophy of Michel Henry, which again is an unmistakable point of reference for Mickel's own undertaking, was conspicuously dismissive of the idea that our individual selfhood bears any essential relation to our earthly parents. In Marion's opinion, this idiosyncrasy of Henry's phenomenology of selfhood and intersubjectivity is a feature of the latter's having been orphaned by his own father at a young age. Mickel explores this crucial but overlooked aspect of our identity that Henry's phenomenology, and that of others, has not taken up to the extent that it could be. For although Levinas and others have done well to emphasize the fundamental way in which we are bound to others, there has been relatively little systematic examination of the specific relation between parent and child. In other words, Mickel's is a work of phenomenological philosophy in its own right, because it thematizes what has heretofore gone concealed or unnoticed in other works of the genre. And although it is written from the perspective of one who is himself a parent, like any good bit of phenomenological philosophy, the analysis on offer transcends the particularity of its author, by bringing to light essential structures of existence that can be appreciated by everyone, regardless of his own circumstances.

If these brief remarks go to show how relatively easy a task it is to locate Mickel's essay in the phenomenological space to which it belongs, what of its broader horizons, particularly that of theology? To put it differently, to what extent is this work theological also? And, assuming that it is so, to some degree, at least, does that fact undermine, or at least complicate, its claim to be a work of philosophy? These are questions that are impossible to avoid. It is not my place to settle them on behalf of its author. As it happens, the work itself is more than capable of defending itself on that score. What, however, one might wonder, are we to make of instances of adoption? Or what of cases in which one believes oneself to be the biological parent of one's child, but is in fact mistaken? Does the analysis of fatherhood inform our understanding of motherhood as well? Does its account of parenthood shed light on what it is to be a son or daughter? If Mickel's brief but dense essay is sure to raise these unanswered questions, that fact is a testament to the work's having extended the phenomenological gaze into terrain which till now remained unseen. The thorough sketch it provides of the phenomenon establishes a framework within which these further questions can begin to be fruitfully addressed.

What should be noted here by way of conclusion, I think, is that the work's bold, but thoughtful, decision to use the term "soul" for the child's mode of appearing, and whose account of the phenomenon of fatherhood cannot help but provoke further theological reflections on the nature of God the Father, is a great merit, rather than a fault, of the work. As the reader will find, the essay's terminology is not to be discounted as a hyperbolic rhetorical flight of fancy. By means of the vocabulary it uses, Mickel brings into language the contours of the phenomena that the essay's careful train of reflections highlights.

Every work of phenomenology is a sending. Its voyage is one whose destination the author himself recognizes he cannot anticipate, for there's no telling where it will land, nor any telling what message it will fully convey, for there is no way of foreseeing who exactly will come to read it. It now having found its way to you, may its words find safe harbor in your hands!

Steven DeLay

Acknowledgments

THANKS ARE IN ORDER first to Creston Davis and the magnificent work he has done making the Global Center for Advanced Studies the school that it is. At a time in my life when I thought my financial and family situation more or less ruled out the possibility of continuing my graduate studies, GCAS's unique model provided a viable way for me to finish my master's degree, and to get a truly world-class education along the way. Thank you, Creston, for your generosity in supporting me and my intellectual interests through the whole process, and for attending always to the effects my education could or would have on me not just as an intellectual but as a human person.

Steven DeLay has also been an invaluable help to me as I have tried to wade my way into the world of French phenomenology. Thank you for offering your time, effort, and thoughtfulness so freely. Thank you as well for your wise guidance through the dense material in our guided readings course on French phenomenology, and for introducing me to the work of so many fine thinkers, especially to your beloved Jean-Louis Chrétien.

To my good friends and siblings in the faith, Michael Ceragioli and Allie Tao, I am most grateful for your intellectual and spiritual companionship. You have been good friends, and a lot of fun, too. Thank you for showing me the many merits of loose-leaf tea and matcha, and for challenging me to always envision a more spacious catholicity. I only hope that our paths continue to interweave so richly in the years ahead.

My faith communities help keep me grounded, prone as I am to wandering off into lonely abstractions and vain ambitions. Thank you to our missional community for your faithfulness as friends. Chad, Dylana, Ben, Brigid, Tiffany, Kris, Allison, and Aaron—I am forever grateful for your company, and for the ways our community always settles each of us back down into the mundane joys of belonging.

I would be remiss to pass over our friends at Saints Hill Church. Emily, Alex, Breanna, Austin, all the leadership team—you have kept the Protestant heart alive in this Catholic convert and continually show me what it is to love Christ with abandon.

And for my friends at my once-home parish of St. Michael the Archangel, I am indebted to you all for showing me what a vibrant Catholic community looks like. I confess I was starting to wonder if such a thing exists anymore. Fr. Ignacio, Ciarán, Elena, Michael and Allie (again), Sigmund, Alex, Tom, Michael Rewers, Sr. Teresa—thanks to you for nurturing my fledgling faith by your own patient, steady (and much more mature) faith.

I could not miss mentioning the wonderful people at Wipf and Stock Publishers, too numerous to name them all. Thank you especially to Charlie Collier and Robin Parry for your encouragement and advice as I navigated new terrain trying to acquire books in philosophy and theology. Throughout the publication process of this book, too, Robin was most encouraging, insightful, and helpful. Thanks once again, Robin. Thanks also to the rest of the editorial team—Michael Thomson, K. C. Hanson, and Rodney Clapp—for your hospitality at my first AAR/SBL conference. But thank you most of all to Jimmy Stock and Jim Tedrick for taking a chance on a confused twenty-something who was turning wrenches when he wanted to be churning through books. You have given me so much to be thankful for in these last five-plus years.

Thank you as well to my parents, who have always journeyed with me as unflinchingly as they could through my most vulnerable times. Mom and Dad, you both taught me how to love. Thank you for trusting me through all the unexpected turns I have taken and continue to take.

My in-laws also deserve mention. You have both been a major source of support for Meredith and me. Thank you for the countless hours of babysitting, Danna, and thank you both for all your affections for your granddaughters.

Most importantly, Meredith, Poppy, and Eloise. Any scholarly accomplishments I might accrue mean absolutely nothing if I have not loved you three down to the bone. I would throw it all away for you guys. Meredith, thank you for putting up with me all these years and for sticking with a man who was far more eccentric and nerdy than you ever bargained for. May we always find our home with one another.

And Poppy and Eloise, this one is for you, my loves. You two are pure gifts, and you will always have a safe place in my arms. May you always trust that your daddy will put his face out in any weather for you, at a moment's notice.

Introduction

I SHOULD MAKE ONE thing clear at the outset: this book is borne in large part from my own experience parenting my now four-year-old daughter. What follows is not first an abstract exercise performed at a remove from the father–child relationship, but is rather a series of reflections that arose for me in those first years of fatherhood. These reflections were aided along by a host of books that helped me to find words for my experience as a father and provided models for how to think my relationship with my daughter. In short, the philosophical meditations occurred both when my nose was buried in a book in the wee hours of the morning as well as when my arms held my sobbing daughter close (also in the wee hours of the morning). My thinking found its way into my life as a parent, and my life as a parent found its way into my thinking.

Because of the intimately personal experience from which these musings emerged—that is, my own situation as the young father of a very young child—the text below is largely focused on describing parental responsibility most especially for the *young* child. The phenomenology of fatherhood contained here is therefore also autobiographical in many ways. It is my effort to faithfully describe my experience parenting my oldest daughter through the early years of her life. Though the topic is personal for me in nature, and though my explorations here come from the fabric of my own life, I am confident that every parent will find something in these pages that resonates with their own experience of parenthood. To say this phenomenological account of fatherhood emerges from my own autobiography is not to say that what you hold in your hands is really a memoir. Nor does it mean that I do not attempt to portray phenomena that would have a wide philosophical applicability for anyone in the position of parent or child. Nowhere do I use my daughter's name, and if I lapse into personal narrative, it is never for longer than a sentence or two. My intention is rather an exploration that takes place at a truly philosophical level, by which I mean at the level of concepts, even if I am always scrupulous to keep the concepts' utmost fidelity to my lived experience. (Alas, an impossible goal, but one we must nonetheless aim for.) I speak most often of "the child," "the father," "the father–child relationship," and occasionally of "I," "me," or "my daughter." I intend by this an interplay of the particular and the universal, and a way of getting to the universal through the particular, even if I never come out and say something like, "*This, and only this,* is fatherhood."

Down in the subterrane of this phenomenological account, the astute reader may note a kind of unfolding pathography of the neuroses that the responsible parent might tend towards. Indeed, it is true that this work grew out of my own grapplings with such neurotic impulses. Here I am thinking of a host of "symptoms" the parent can experience rising up within themselves, including but certainly not limited to phenomena like the desire to control the child's life to the maximal extents, the excessively felt need to protect the child from any and all harm, obsessive fears around the child and their well-being, etc., etc. This pathographical subterrane is in large measure autobiographical, too, emerging from my own experience as a parent with obsessive tendencies.

From the moment my daughter was born, I could not escape the immediate sense of her great existential fragility. She emerged from her mother's womb breathless, a bluish-purple across her face, no voice, no cries. The nurses had to resuscitate her with an infant bag-valve mask for thirteen minutes as I stood next to her bassinet and held her tiny hand, afraid I would accidentally squeeze her hand too firmly and hurt her fragile little fingers. I wanted to speak to her, to offer her some gentle and reassuring words in this most frightening moment, but instead I found myself mute, standing there in a state of shock, embarrassed at my inadequacy, feeling utterly helpless.

Eventually the nurses were able to stabilize her breathing, and then we could finally swaddle her up in a blanket, hold her close to our chests, and sing hymns to her. Only then were my wife and I able to settle in and watch our precious new daughter now peacefully sleeping. And only then did the adrenaline drain out and the terror of what we had just undergone come home for us. Amidst the waves of relief crashing over us, we had no words and could do nothing but weep.

This was of course just one of many instances—the most frightening one, to be sure—in which I have experienced my own visceral response to my daughter's existential vulnerability. From this moment have followed all the usual sufferings of childhood which rend the parent's heart: inconsolable wailing in the deeps of night, stomach aches and suppositories, crashes and scrapes, nightmares and fear of monsters. This is not even to mention the constancy and pace of change that the young child undergoes in their early development, the brute fact of the father's inability to capture his beloved from the relentless passage of time, his constitutional inability to prepare for all the phenomena that his child's immersion within the pains and joys of their own finitude will bring him. He does not want to accept the fact that he does not—indeed, *cannot*—know what he is doing. No matter his fittedness for the parental task, he knows deep down that he is in some serious way, at the level of his human constitution, always unfit for the task.

It was from these experiences that my thoughts on the father's experience of his young child's passage through time arose. What became more and more apparent to me was that this site of the father's sense of responsibility for his child is precisely the place where the child's finitude and the father's finitude meet, and that this meeting place is perhaps the highest form of love in the relationship between father and child. A communion is obtained there at the father's finitudinal limits, there where the father offers his own presence, however inadequate, at the altar of his child's vulnerability, that most sacred exposure which is the child's outness in the world. This communion is nothing more than a mutual exposure in which the father braves the weather, whatever the conditions, in which his child exists. What follows in the pages below is a kind of dance around these themes, an exploration of the father's experience of the excess that arrives for him in his child's face (what I will call *the child's soul*), his sense of responsibility for this precious soul, which sits exposed to the elements of life out in the world, and the sacrifices he makes—particularly in the late modern setting—for the sake of his child's soul.

Before we begin our description of these phenomena that arise in fatherhood, though, we should pause to make a few important notes on method, particularly about the epistemological tradition from which this book draws. To understand the approach of my own phenomenological work here, we will first have to understand how knowing and knowledge figure in the thought of the major historical figures in phenomenology.[1]

---

1. Unfortunately, it was only after writing the manuscript for this book that I was also introduced to the abundant feminist literature on motherhood, childhood, and the family. Thanks to Natalie Carnes for directing me to this literature, especially to the work of Adrienne Rich, Sara Ruddick, and Bonnie Miller-McLemore. Time constraints

Three such figures would be Edmund Husserl, Martin Heidegger, and Emmanuel Levinas. The latter actually went to Freiburg to study under Husserl, and when Husserl retired, continued with Heidegger, who had been Husserl's protégé and who then filled Husserl's former post at the university after his retirement. None of these three pioneers in phenomenology fit neatly anywhere on the spectrum of viewpoints represented in contemporary epistemology, a subfield which is much more prominent in the arena of analytic philosophy. Indeed, the philosopher Henry Pietersma has pointed out that at least Heidegger is "on record" as having rejected epistemology.[2] As Pietersma argues, however, one cannot escape epistemology entirely, and so we find in Heidegger's work an *implicit* epistemology that is however never laid out *explicitly*. If there is one among these three who is nearest to the edges of the analytic world of epistemology, though, it is surely Husserl, whose project was in many ways to construct a theory of knowledge that could account for the problems of intentionality and the natural attitude and the need for the phenomenological reduction in order to approach what he thinks of as "pure" knowledge.

We might say that Husserl sets the tone for phenomenological accounts of belief and knowledge by attending to the *inner experience* of beliefs and knowledge. While Husserl will attend to matters such as justification, veracity, and so forth, he approaches these questions through an experiential frame. He wants to consider the inner workings of "the believing subject" as he processes "extrinsic information" according to certain beliefs he holds.[3] Husserl does so by a methodology of *description*, which becomes one of the hallmarks of the phenomenological tradition. Husserlian phenomenology thus seeks to describe how the subject maps external phenomena within the web of beliefs he holds. For Husserl, knowledge is in some sense the act of the subject observing the process by which he or she cognitively receives objects and places them within an inner world of beliefs. This has hints of coherentism, but in this case the emphasis is less on establishing the structure of knowledge itself

---

kept me from incorporating these important thinkers in this "essay," which is instead a focused conversation mostly with European—especially French—phenomenology, but I do hope to engage with this body of feminist writings on motherhood and family life in my future work. Carnes's own book on motherhood is itself an excellent (and beautifully written) contribution in this vein. See Carnes, *Motherhood*.

2. Pietersma, *Phenomenological Epistemology*, viii.

3. Pietersma, *Phenomenological Epistemology*, 5.

and more on describing the internal, cognitive structure of the subject's knowledge-building (or more precisely, knowledge-situating). Husserl's epistemological approach is thus thoroughly focused on the internal and the mental. In fact, he is wont to agree with Descartes on the "givenness of mental representations."[4] For him, epistemology cannot begin from external data but must start with what the subject "provides for itself and posits as primal."[5] And in Husserl's mind, the apex of such internal workings must be a transcendental viewpoint that subordinates the manner in which the subject receives the phenomenon. This transcendental viewpoint is the "absolute consciousness" in which the subject observes the way she *intends* the object within an internal web of beliefs and so is able to suspend such intentionality and so receive the object more purely.[6] Here follows less of the aforementioned mapping of the object within a web of beliefs and more the description of the object as it gives itself to the subject.

While Husserl thus positions knowledge as primary in the phenomenological method, Heidegger views it as a product of our "being-in-the-world." What is primary for Heidegger is not epistemology, but ontology. Therefore, for him knowledge flows from the subject's existence among entities, from the subject's placement within a world in which objects are always already given to be used rather than observed. The subject is always *in* the world, *involved* in his environment, operating in a *practical* mode, *using* objects that necessarily give themselves to the subject as tools to be used. In other words, there is no neutral ground to stand on from which to observe objects at a distance. One cannot observe things in the world disinterestedly but rather always approaches them with interest, with "care." Key for Heidegger, too, is what he terms the "ontological difference." This is his claim that "the being of entities can be clarified only by reference to something which is not itself an entity."[7] For Heidegger, this something is "Dasein," which eludes precise definition

---

4. Pietersma, *Phenomenological Epistemology*, 55.

5. Pietersma, *Phenomenological Epistemology*, 55.

6. Here I use "intend" and "intentionality" in Husserl's technical meaning of the term: as an act of consciousness that is secondary to the thing itself (in itself). We could also speak of the difference between the thing itself and how the thing *appears to me*, or how it *gives itself to me* (in my consciousness). Thus opens a question of the possible artificiality and second-handedness of such "intentional" mental phenomena, which may be somehow less authentic or less rich than the thing in its own right.

7. Pietersma, *Phenomenological Epistemology*, 88.

but which could be more or less adequately summed up as *human be-ing*, particularly its being-*there*—or as we said earlier, its "being-in-the-world—but also its "being-with," "being-for," "being-towards-death," and "being-towards-potentiality." In other words, knowing happens only within being, and being thus dictates the character of knowing insofar as knowing is always knowing in the *context* constitutive of human being-in-the-world. Heidegger's fundamental critique of Husserl, then, is that he has not gone far enough, because he has arrived at "consciousness" but has failed to go on and ask about the *being* of consciousness.

Building on the work of his predecessors, Husserl and Heidegger, Levinas problematizes what seems to him the solipsism of their accounts of the subject's cognitional experience. He does so by intrusion of the other into the subject's frame. It is not that Husserl and Heidegger do not consider the other at all in their accounts; indeed, far from it. Rather, it is that for them the other is but one piece of the puzzle, whereas for Levinas it is the only lens by which one can see truth at all. The other intrudes and disrupts the subject's enjoyment (*jouissance*) of objects and the subject's (typically unwitting) attempts to view the other too as an object of enjoyment. In this way Levinas refigures Husserl's idea of inten-tionality as fundamentally about the subject's approach towards objects as affectation, or more precisely, as enjoyment and nourishment.[8] The mental representation is then always operating in the mode of desiring and seeking comfort, the feeling of need and of need's satisfaction. Only by the other's intrusion can the subject overcome this intentionality of enjoyment, since the other who meets the I always comes with a face, that is, a face that bespeaks the other's vulnerability, his nakedness, his being-unto-death. The face cannot hide this nakedness which is "more naked than nudity."[9] This face of the other issues a call to the subject, a call that demands a response, that demands responsibility.

Still, we should ask: How exactly does overcoming the intentionality of enjoyment by the other's intrusion in any way lead the subject closer to truth? Has not this movement simply problematized the subject's inten-tionality of enjoyment without then offering a subsequent, constructive movement that would lead the subject towards truth? Here Levinas will insist on the inseparable connection between *justification* (of beliefs) and *justice*. A more just justification, in Levinas's view, begins with the subject's

8. Levinas, *Totality and Infinity*, 127.
9. Levinas, *Otherwise Than Being*, 88.

posture of self-criticism before the other.[10] The subject must humble herself as pupil of the other who is her teacher. (Here as elsewhere we see the Jewishness of Levinas's thought, particularly the *Talmudic* dimensions of his philosophy.) Without this submission to the other's demand on the subject, the subject will always think the other by her own resources, will always think the other in terms of *more of the same* (as me). To know the other is to let the other be radically other and thus to receive him as he truly is. This mode of justice before the other thereby opens onto discourse, in which the subject actually receives a teaching exterior to herself and so enters a plane of intersubjectivity beyond more of the same.[11]

In what follows, I will bring some of the epistemological tools Levinas and his two phenomenological predecessors have offered and extend these into the terrain of the theological turn that has taken place and continues apace in French (and now American) phenomenology.[12] This means my book will also engage with phenomenologists like Jean-Luc Marion, Claude Romano, Jean-Yves Lacoste, and Emmanuel Falque. Much like Heidegger and Levinas, I will subordinate epistemology to a particular iteration of ontology. Moving from Heidegger's being-in-the-world, being-towards-potentiality, and being-towards-death and what we could call Levinas's being-captive-to-the-other, I will move into what we could call a liturgical ontology, by which I mean something like an ontology oriented to the sacred. I will thus work from the clearing that thinkers like Lacoste and Falque[13] have worked so diligently to open, a spacious place where philosophy and theology are brought back into mutual dialogue and can enrich one another. Like Falque, then, I will embrace the "backlash" or the "return shock" of theology onto phenomenology and so present a phenomenology-in-the-faith.[14]

That is not to say that what you will find here is a Christian theology cloaked in the garb of phenomenological philosophy. Far from it; indeed, you may well have trouble spotting anything specifically Christian in the pages that follow. What I aim to undertake here is not so much a

10. Levinas, *Totality and Infinity*, 83.

11. Levinas, *Totality and Infinity*, 89.

12. For a most helpful introduction to this French "theological turn," see DeLay, *Phenomenology in France*. Another good resource here is Donald Wallenfang's Cascade Companion on the topic. See Wallenfang, *Phenomenology*.

13. On the renewed relationship between philosophy and theology, see especially Lacoste, *From Theology to Theological Thinking*; Falque, *Crossing the Rubicon*.

14. Again, see Falque, *Crossing the Rubicon*.

Christian philosophy of fatherhood, but rather a phenomenological description of fatherhood that is open to the kind of sacredness of the *imago Dei* within the human person that Christianity teaches. If it resembles Christian theology in any way, then, it is first and foremost a *theological anthropology*, but one presented without all the particulars of Christian revelation, even if the very foundation of the description undertaken is Christian through and through. The primary objective here is a faithful adherence to the experiential textures of fatherhood. But because I am a practicing Christian, the reader should know that my faith colors every aspect of this experiential topography of fatherhood, such that my practice of the Christian religion spreads its light into every nook and cranny of my experience parenting my young daughter. The astute reader will of course pick up on this invisible scaffolding of the religion which holds up my description of the father–child relationship, particularly in the below discussions around the child's *soul* and the father's *sacrifice*. It is perhaps no mystery, then, that these two considerations (the soul and sacrifice) serve as bookends at the beginning and end of this book.

As I say, the book opens with a first section on the child's soul as shown in their face. Here we will lay the groundwork for what it means to think about such religious concepts as "soul" in a post-religious age. What can such a thing as "soul" mean in today's world? Is this not the naïve God-talk of mythological ages long past? However, by thinking through Marion's notion of the "saturated phenomenon" and his exposition of the face, or what he sometimes also calls the *icon*, we will attend to that strange and powerful infinity which the father experiences in the child's face, and how some invisible excess beyond words seems to reach out from the incarnate and visible face of the child. I will argue here that the child's face *speaks* the child's soul, that the child's soul comes to the father *through* the child's eyes. This look from the child's eyes speaks much more substantially than words and yet commences in the father an endless hermeneutic in which he tries to patiently describe that which he knows he can never contain within words. And the task of such a patient description requires a posture of awestruck attention, the kind of *attention* that the child's face demands, making its call for an impossible but requisite wonder and respect proper to the infinity that issues from the face.

In the second chapter, I then look at the ways in which the child's soul can only manifest visibly within the confines of human finitude, and at the ethical call that issues from the child's face in such a state of existential flux. Here we will move from Marion to Levinas and Romano, thinking in terms of the former's use of *the face* as opening on to an infinity, but also, because of the finitude in which the face finds itself, as always subject to change, suffering, and finally death. Romano's treatment of *the event* also proves most helpful here, particularly as I explore the reconfiguring impact of the event on the child's psyche, how the child must *advene*, borrowing Romano's neologism, to the events—even (especially!) the traumatic ones—that visit the child and that the father is so often helpless in defending the child from. With the child in such a setting as this, their finitude leaving them exposed to the evential violences of time, the responsive father discerns a call to break off in some measure from his own attachments and enjoyments in life in order to be more fully attentive and available to his child. In this giving up—or at least relativizing—of his own projects and delights, this giving himself away to and for his child, he finds a new and vocational sense of self. That is, his life becomes vocative; he is now the addressed one, the designated one, the one called out. He and he alone, he in his singularity, arrives for his child with a "Here I am."

Today, however, this doubled call to *attention* (Marion) and *responsibility* (Levinas) sounds from the child's face only amidst all the noise and clamor of the late modern world. Which is to say that modernity to some significant degree actually mutes, or at least muffles, the call of the child's face. This muting of the child's call in modernity is the topic of our third chapter. We begin this section, though, with a brief survey of the important phenomenological critique of modernity found in the work of Michel Henry, who exposes the modern world's penchant for objectivity. Henry sees this feature as invading each and every corner, however remote, of modern life. To this incisive critique, I will contribute my own brief analysis of modernity's increasing devotion to speed and consumption. The ever-expanding infiltration of these in modern life, I argue, erodes the father's *attentional* and *ascetical* faculties, and creates at both the societal and the personal levels an appetitional maelstrom. This maelstrom, this appetitive overload, indeed comes to exhaust the father's time and energy, leaving little to no room (or capacity) for the patient and quiet attention for which the child's face calls. The father, then, must work to cultivate within himself a capacity for attention and asceticism, but he must do so within a sociohistorical environment that relentlessly works against such a cultivation of the virtues involved in intersubjective responsibility.

The fourth chapter of the book then traverses the tricky terrain of sacrifice as it pertains to the father's care for his child. Here we explore the father's confrontation with the limits of his love for his child, limits that his own finitude imposes on him, those places he is constitutionally unable to access, where his child is exposed alone and out on their own to all manner of possible traumas. The literary example of the Akedah, or the binding of Isaac, and the filmic example of Tarkovsky's *The Sacrifice* enliven what I mean here by the term *the unthinkable sacrifice*. This sacrifice takes place at that site of intimacy, that mutual exposure made possible by the utmost trust, which is a communion of the father's soul and the child's soul. For all the joys the father experiences in this intimacy with his child, there is always at the edges of his mind also the threat of some unwelcome invasion or violation of his child's fundamental exposedness, an existential vulnerability that the child offers to him as father so freely, laying the child's vulnerability bare most poignantly in this moment of intimacy with me, their father.

While most parents gratefully do not have to make the kind of unthinkable sacrifice that Tarkovsky's protagonist performs and Abraham almost performs, most of us are nevertheless faced with unsettling *thoughts* of such an unthinkable sacrifice, of some unthinkable trauma visiting the child and by its brute force battering their innocence. This could be any manner of trauma: a severe illness, some form of abuse, a serious accident, natural disaster, war conditions, the loss of a loved one, and on and on. Romano re-emerges here with his description of the experience of terror, which I apply to the father's confrontation with terrorizing intrusive thoughts around the possibility of some significant harm befalling his child. Jordan Peele's *Get Out* provides a nice filmic image of the experience of terror as Romano (and I) mean it and homes our analysis in on a concrete example that we can relate to the visceral fears that visit the father. Weathering such psychic conditions and accepting them as part and parcel of the experience of fatherhood, the father is able to make of them an act of love for his child. These become a kind of psychic trauma that the father allows himself to undergo in an act of self-exposure at the limits of his ability to care for his child. It is this willingness to be exposed to the elements together with his child that constitutes the far edges of a father's surrender to whatever conditions his love for the child may require him to live within. And this surrender to the task of self-exposure is nothing less than the father's loving offering of his own vulnerability there at the feet of his child's always greater vulnerability.

1

Facing the Child's Soul

"What kind of light is that? Oh, it is the light within, the light that shines
in all the eyes we meet, known and unknown. The eyes of strangers, for
instance on board a packed bus on an autumn afternoon, emit a faint light,
more like a barely perceptible glimmer in their grimy faces, and what it
reveals is hardly more than that they are alive. But the moment those little
lanterns of life are turned towards you, and you look into them, what you
see is a particular human being. Maybe you take notice of them, maybe not,
in the course of a life we gaze into thousands of eyes, most of them slipping
by unperceived, but then suddenly there is something there, in those eyes,
something you want and which you would do almost anything to be close
to. What is it? For it isn't the pupils you are seeing then, not the irises nor
the whites of the eyes. It is the soul, the archaic light of the soul the eyes are
filled with, and to gaze into the eyes of the one you love when love is at its
most powerful belongs among the highest joys."

—KARL OVE KNAUSGAARD[1]

WE BEGIN WITH THE question of the child's soul and what this idea of
soul might mean in the post-religious and now post-secular context we
find ourselves in. It might strike some as rather odd to even speak of such
a thing as the soul today. What I mean here by soul is not necessarily
directly equivalent to the kind of traditional doctrines of soul one finds

1. Knausgaard, *Autumn*, 224.

in, say, Platonism or Christianity. That is not to diminish the legitimacy of such traditional notions of the soul in any way, only to say that this way of thinking the soul is not what I undertake here. What I aim to do instead is to think the child's soul according to the existential heft of their life as a human person. The term serves here less a religious function and more an experiential function common perhaps to all human persons. This is the idea of the child's soul as the father's experience of the finality of the child's life, the fundamental importance of this child, the weight of glory that their eyes speak to me as father.[2] It is something akin to what Emmanuel Levinas means by "the face" and Jean-Luc Marion "the icon." The maneuver at hand, thus, is to *face the child's soul*, as it were, that is, to think the child's soul according to the phenomena that emerge for the father as he gazes upon his child's face.

The next question we must ask, then, is what this might mean today, to *face* the child's soul. What gives us any right, after all, to speak of a "soul" in a world that no longer seems to believe in such things? And yet even the most atheistic reduction cannot erase the sublimity we sometimes experience as we look into the endless recesses of another's eyes. Some excess in the child's face, when we "have eyes to see," reaches us and affects us. Facing the child's soul, then, may mean something like attending to the child with a certain contemplative posture. This task requires a patient attention and an openness to the excess that may unfold for us as we gaze upon the child's face. Inversely, facing the child's soul would also entail thinking the child's soul precisely *through* their face. In other words, that the child's face *speaks* their soul to me in some way. The face here provides an access point to some infinite we encounter most poignantly when the face comes to us as an experience of the sublime, in whatever measure. (It may be only the slightest hint of sublimity, or it may totally consume us.) As Levinas would say, the face serves in this way as a point of dilation opening onto some infinite.

Marion's rich concept of the "saturated phenomenon" proves most helpful in our consideration of the child's face. Indeed, the face, or what he sometimes calls the "icon," is one of Marion's five saturated phenomena, all of which he outlines within the pages of his *In Excess* (and elsewhere, we should note). The notion of the saturated phenomenon is one that, to my knowledge, Marion himself developed as a way to describe that which eludes the conceptual. These are the phenomena in which,

---

2. I borrow the terms *finality* and *importance* from Henry Bugbee and *the weight of glory* from C. S. Lewis. See Bugbee, *Inward Morning*; Lewis, *Weight of Glory*.

"to the contrary of poor and common phenomena, intuition gives (itself) in exceeding what the concept (signification, intentionality, aim, and so on) can foresee of it and show."[3] We might think of these saturated phenomena as being particularly rich in meaning, indeed as opening up a superabundance of meanings that can never be closed down or upon which the lid can never be shut. Marion will at times also speak of these saturated phenomena as "paradoxes." By this he simply means that they "do not give themselves in a univocal display, available and mastered, according to a doxa,"[4] but rather that they give themselves in a surplus of meanings that we interpret, however inadequately, via an "endless hermeneutic." As we will see later, the child's face opens up just such an endless hermeneutic.

The child's face may in fact appear to us more readily as such a saturated phenomenon than any adult's face would. Some mysterious quality in the child's face always renders their soul unguardedly, without any layer of guile blocking its manifestation. The child cannot help but bare their soul in their eyes. Even when the child is shy, their eyes somehow speak to us unguardedly. The child seems somehow unable to turn off, so to speak, this glimmer of transparency which issues from their eyes. Their face is always uncovered, coming forth as an exposure of their soul which they at no time chose to expose. This quality of the child's face, its guileless exposedness, bears a special capacity for affecting the onlooker, the one who sees the child's face. The adult is more prone to feel affected, reached somehow, by the face of a child than that of another adult. My wife and I have sometimes commented to each other how, before having children, so few people would say hello to us or stop to converse with us when we walked through the park near our house. But now that we have a child, it is remarkable to watch how many people will smile at our daughter, wave and say hello to her, stop to tell her how beautiful she is, and so on. Something about the child's face draws us in in a special way. There is some excess here that speaks to us and moves us. It calls most of all for our attention.

There is, in fact, something of a sacramental character, or an iconicity, to the child's face. The child's face reveals some invisible mystery, bringing this invisible mystery into visibility, to the extent that it can. Marion will often speak in the pages of *In Excess* of the visible both

3. Marion, *In Excess*, 112.
4. Marion, *In Excess*, 112.

concealing and revealing an invisibility, or what Marion is wont to call, using his native French tongue, *"l'invu"* (the unseen). The invisible here takes on the stature, we might say, of the visible, precisely in order to give itself as visible. In Marion's words: "The invisible only breaks forth into day *constrained to finitude*—crowned with an invisible by default, *l'invu.*"[5] The saturated phenomenon of the child's face hides to some extent the invisible, its great excess, even as its visible manifestation paradoxically gestures towards just this invisible beyond concept, this insurmountable and uncapturable excess. This is why we choose to speak of the child's face as revealing a *mystery*, for what it reveals is beyond the capacities of our comprehension. This mystery, this excess, overflows all conceptual containment. Thus, it reveals in the mode of the icon, which is perhaps just to say that the child's face bears a truly religious significance, that it gestures towards an image of humanity beyond all concepts.

The face for Marion (and Levinas) shows itself always as a gesture towards excess, towards the eternal. The face therefore opens up what Marion calls an "endless hermeneutic" which follows from the infinity of meanings flowing from said face. In the words of Marion, "It [the icon] must be allowed, then, to overflow with many meanings, an infinity of meanings, each equally legitimate and rigorous, without managing either to unify them or to organize them."[6] The visible face of the child, then, both conceals and reveals an invisible always overflowing endlessly with meaning, an overflow that can never be scooped up and contained, bottled back up, or managed. And yet the paradox here is that the child's face also at the same time gives an infinity of meanings even precisely *within its finitude.* The changes wrought by the events it undergoes make the child's face always different, always new, never the same twice. Here opens what we might call the infinity of the face's finitude, which arrives parallel to the infinity qua infinity the face conceals (and reveals). The child's face gives itself anew with each moment, each look, showing the surplus of its finitude.

It is clear, then, that the icon of the child's face bears a richness far beyond what any concept could contain. This very richness is indeed what makes the other's face both unobjectifiable and unmasterable for Marion. "I cannot have vision of these [saturated] phenomena," he writes, "because I cannot constitute them starting from a univocal meaning, and even less

5. Marion, *In Excess*, 105, emphasis mine.
6. Marion, *In Excess*, 112.

produce them as objects."[7] Simply put, I cannot make the child's face into an object. It is perhaps possible to think the child's face as object, to schematize it as such, but to do so is to enact a kind of violence upon the thing itself, the face that gives itself, and that gives itself all the more as I bracket its objectification all the more. To make the icon into an object, or even to think it as a "univocal display," is to already think it, as we quoted earlier, as "available and mastered, according to a *doxa*."[8] But the child's face gives far beyond objectivity, gives in some way even infinity, gives what I can never master, what I can never schematize or rationalize. In fact, as Levinas constantly reminds us, it is actually the other's face itself that is my master in the scenario of the face-to-face. I do not determine the child's face, but rather the child's face determines me.

It remains unclear, though, what exactly this unmasterable excess is. If we are not careful, we run the risk here of a great philosophical imprecision and perhaps of a too-romantic description of the child's face. John Milbank, for instance, has criticized Marion's work for always lapsing into a rather "blank sublimity"[9] under the banner of the "saturated phenomenon." We may have even given the impression in this book of waxing poetic about the iconicity of the child's face without first exercising the philosophical rigor necessary for truly thinking this face. We should also ask, though: Does the vagueness of this sublimity make it any less real? Does its indeterminancy mean that it bears no existential veracity? It is, after all, the overwhelming potency of the child's look, their eyes, that makes the child's face so hard to pin down with any univocal or metaphysical precision.

And yet this face of the child calls for evermore description. It is indeed an endless hermeneutic. Most simply, we can describe the child's face as both concealing and revealing a *mystery*, and we can furthermore say that this mystery is best described as the child's *soul*. What my daughter's face shows is the mystery of her soul, an incomprehensible mystery that nonetheless always speaks to me and always sounds a new word or, better, sings a new note. From her face bursts forth the unending song of her soul. Something here gives off some scent of the divine, some thoroughgoing goodness that can never be effaced nor lost. This mystery

7. Marion, *In Excess*, 113.

8. Marion, *In Excess*, 112.

9. Milbank used this phrase in reference to Marion during an interview I conducted with him for Wipf and Stock Publishers' *The Theology Mill* podcast. See the bibliography entry for Mickel, "Luminaries."

flows forth from the child's face in the form of nothing less than the visibility of an unsurpassable invisible, the incarnation of the child's soul in the impenetrable depths of their pupils. This phenomenon of the invisible made visible (in some small part) eludes the objectivity of definition, which would only be a useless effort to contain the uncontainable depths of that complex creature called the human person. The force of this phenomenon breaks through and thus breaks down any consideration of the child on the level of objecthood, along with any description of the child conducted at a purely material or biological level. Scientific objectivity, quite simply, cannot touch this phenomenon of which we speak. It lacks more than anything the spiritual resources to do so, the kind of vision that the child's soul calls for.

At this point, though, we must not fall into the trap of simply chalking the child's soul up to a mystery and leaving it at that. Phenomenology gifts us with the task of describing such sublimities, if only in an exploratory manner and always with a view towards respecting the ultimate unknowability of such a mystery as the soul. We must ask, then, what we mean to say when we use a phrase like "the child's soul." What are we trying to describe when we use this word *soul*, particularly when we use it in relation to the child and the deepest reaches of the child's interiority?

In response to such a question, there are three important facets I would wish to draw out here. The first and second are (1) the soul as the largeness of a singular human spirit, its immeasurable excess, and (2) the soul's unwavering dynamism. We could even be so bold as to liken the child's soul to a massive underwater cave. There are depths there that one cannot easily access and that prove impossible to map with any precision. We might imagine the child's soul as this kind of cave, which is only dimly lit, a phenomenon that is darker as it is deeper. Its cracks and crevices, its topographical details, ever changing with the ocean's persistent movement, do not make for ready mapping; indeed, one may discover some of these details are more or less impossible to find. And whatever pieces the father finds in this cavernous soul, he must leave intact. These pieces, after all, do not belong to him; they are not something he can break off and take with him. There is a mineness about the constitution of the child's soul that stipulates that it can only ever belong to the child themself. This not only in an ethical sense, but in the sense of the impossibility of the father ever reaching the other side of the child's soul so as to take up residence there, where only the child themself can truly reside, a place over which the child is sovereign and within which the father is constitutionally unable, as a finite and singular human being, to make a home. What we have in the soul, then, is a site of inaccessible depths with unclaimable (and sometimes unreachable) wonders.

This image of the deep underwater cave speaks to both the *enormity* and the *dynamism* of the child's soul. This cave simply penetrates too deep beneath the waters and is too large in scope for, say, a scuba diver, to explore and log all its makeup. Moreover, the diver will discover with each new dive that, though he is still seeing the same cave, it has a new look about it. The ocean's unending movement has changed the face of the cave since the last dive, and will continue to perpetually alter the way the cave appears to the onlooker. And apart from all change, the onlooker will only ever be able to view this cavernous terrain from one angle at a time. Roughly speaking, we can think of the soul of the child as something like this, a phenomenon that arrives for the father in certain moments of peak sensitivity as something powerful and intensely real and thus as an overfullness that he welcomes with whatever stores of love he can muster. But due to the enormity of the child's soul, no number of the father's gazes can ever come close to covering the full breadth and depth of this plenitudinous and dynamic terrain.

The third element we should consider here is the father's sense of the child's soul as something in constant endangerment. This phenomenon that is the child's soul, though displaying glimpses of its enormity and always shifty in its appearance, seems to appear most clearly to the father when it shows its position within human *precarity*, that it always exists within the human situation of risk of danger and death. In its moments of greatest thrownness into finitudinal fragility, its preciousness is somehow made more real for the father. It is an excess beyond all epistemic capture, and yet the father only ever knows this excess as something given over to human and thus finitudinal conditions, in some way passive with respect to the violences of time and event. This soul of the child shows itself most brilliantly when it is in harm's way—which it always is, but at certain times much more obviously than at others. What is perhaps most heartbreaking for the father about the situation of the child's soul, though, is that the father can never adequately secure it nor make it safe. It is in fact an impossible task to protect the child's soul from all harm, and for the father to undertake such a task would only cause the child's soul a different kind of harm anyhow, that of disrespecting or defacing the child's freedom.

So we see, by way of introduction, that the child's soul, as I am think-ing of it on these pages, is marked first by its *enormity*, its *dynamism*, and its *situatedness within human precarity*. This now gives us a first pass at analyzing the phenomenon of the child's soul, some at least tentative holds to grab onto as we explore deep and mysterious underwaters. What follows will, I hope, continue to unfurl this phenomenon that I have al-ready begun to describe, though of course never sufficiently, in the face of a soul which is at bottom bottomless, an impenetrable mystery. (But to linger and to describe is an act of love!—or at least a loving attempt to love all the way down to the bone, a perhaps impossible task but a good and necessary one.)

This also brings us to a first start at describing the nature of the *call* that the child's soul speaks, the demands it makes on the father. These demands consist first of all in the cultivation of a kind of vision, a manner of seeing, or better, to borrow again from Marion, a manner of "envisag-ing" the face of the child. Vision here is first and foremost a mode of attention, what we might think of as a kind of contemplative mode of attention before the mystery of the child's soul. It is the father's manner of approaching the child in all their mystery in a mode of respect and wonder. Here again Marion's descriptive efforts are most helpful:

> [The face's] phenomenality is accomplished when it is made heard (understood), when the weight of its glory weighs upon me, when it inspires respect. *To respect*—to attract sight and at-tention (*-spectare*), of course—but because I feel myself called and held at a distance by the weight of an invisible look, by its si-lent appeal. *To respect* is also understood as the counter-concept of *to look at*.[10]

So, the first facet of the child's call is the injunction to attend, and to attend with respect and wonder. It is this call to attention that com-prises a constitutive feature of parental responsibility, and it is a call to attend without end, to follow the child with my attention in their passage through time. My responsibility here meets the child's finitude, the many contingencies that will make up their life, so many of which I have little to no control over. The call of the child's soul is that I never leave them, no matter what events or conditions may come, that I never turn my back nor leave them all alone to face the sheer force of the events that will in some measure determine their life.

---

10. Marion, *In Excess*, 119.

2

The Child's Finitude

"Up to this point, my role as your mother has been to reduce your pain and to impose myself between you and the world. I have absorbed life's trials to give you a safe and happy space to grow. You have been like your father's seedlings, under a grow-light indoors, protected from harsh winds, hard rains, and hungry snails. But now you are making your way into a less buffered world, finding more of the world's beauty and discovering the way joy comes alloyed with suffering. My job at this point is to trust that the suffering of the world will not extinguish your joy and to recede, just a little, so that you can enter more deeply into the world."

—NATALIE CARNES[1]

THE FATHER'S FACING OF the child's soul, of course, can only be of a soul as appearing within the confines of finitude. If the invisible is made visible, it can only be so according to the world in which the visible manifests itself, that is, according to a world that relentlessly inflicts change upon all that is visible. As citizen in this world of the visible, the child is endlessly subject to change, placed in some respect at the mercy of the event's great force. Here I am following Claude Romano's excellent exposition of the event in his *Event and World*, in which he speaks of the event as something that happens *to* me and before which I am largely passive. In a way, the event re-worlds me by unsettling and reconfiguring my options,

1. Carnes, *Motherhood*, 56.

19

or my possibilities, within the world. It inflicts a violence of sorts in my life, "completely upending my essential possibilities articulated among themselves in a world and so upsetting my own adventure."[2] This *evential violence* which is a constitutive feature of time thus fundamentally alters my experience of myself in the world and my experience of the future that lies before me. I am forced in this way to "advene," as Romano puts it, to this reconfiguration, to accept and adapt to this new reality that the event unfurls. I absorb the event's blunt force, and it irreparably changes me and my world. Now I am the "advenant,"[3] the one who comes to terms with the wake the event leaves behind in my world. In short, the event recasts everything, sparing none. The event thereby reveals the radical contingency that marks my relationship with time.

Childhood is in a special way the era of the event's greatest impact. The child's guileless exposedness, of which we spoke already, leaves the child particularly vulnerable to the event's blunt force, for good and for ill. The child stands completely unarmored in the direct path of the event, having no resources at their disposal to soften its impact. There is consequently a unique plasticity to the child, who absorbs the event with little to no buffer. Not only is the child particularly vulnerable to the event's power; they are also more likely than the adult to be made new by the event, to have their world and their very sense of self recast in the event's wake. This is in part why the events of childhood can be so determinative for the rest of life. The child is in the process of world-construction, discerning their own relation to the world, developing an "attachment style," as the psychotherapists say. The events that make up a childhood produce the child's world and give it meaning. These events are the foundation for the world the child will live within and build upon into their adulthood. The child learns from the event and adapts themself to it, *advenes* to it, reconsidering the fundamental questions that determine their sense of self and their (childlike) relation to the world: Is the world safe or dangerous? Are others trustworthy or untrustworthy? Am I a good or a bad person? Etc., etc.

The father can likewise have a sensitive relationship to the events that appear in his child's life, most especially to those we might call *events of suffering* or even *traumatic events*. Here the father is tasked first with triage and then, if the traumatic impact is severe enough, with aftercare.

---

2. Romano, *Event and World*, 29.

3. Romano, *Event and World*, 29.

Even the smaller traumas of everyday life—falling over and scratching a knee, missing one's mother or father at bedtime, experiencing digestive pains, etc.—can upend the young child for a moment or a day or a string of days. For the father these smaller traumas can rend the heart, too, particularly as they seem to pile up on each other in frequent occurrences over time. It is hard to watch a young child suffer, especially one's own child. And of course there are the larger traumas that every responsible father most fears will visit his child: a serious illness, abuse at the hands of some other, or simply the pileup of smaller related traumas that together accrue a great evential force (as in the case of chronic bouts with bullying at school, for instance). Equally torturous for the father is the fear that his own neuroses will accumulate in such a way as to unintentionally deliver a decisive evential blow to the child and configure the child's world accordingly. Regardless of the details, however, the father is inescapably confronted with the reality of suffering and trauma in his child's life, so much of which he cannot prevent from occurring, much as he might like to substitute himself and stand in for his child in those moments.

Why do events like these affect us as adults with such force when a child is involved, though? What is it about the child that renders me as a father so affectable? To answer this question, we must turn again to our consideration of the child's face, this time, however, with Levinas rather than Marion. For his part, Levinas often speaks of the face in quite vivid images of existential vulnerability and neediness. He writes, for instance: "The disclosing of a face is nudity, non-form, abandon of the self, ageing, dying, *more naked than nudity*."[4] To envisage the other's face is for Levinas to witness its givenness to suffering and death, to face unfiltered the piercing reality of the other's vulnerability before the evential violences of time. The other's eyes speak, as it were, this vulnerability in a special way, and so Levinas will also talk of "the total nudity of his [the other's] *defenceless eyes* . . . the nudity of the absolute openness [to suffering and death]."[5] And as I argued earlier, the child is especially exposed to such violences of time. The answer to our question, then, is that the child renders me as father uniquely affectable first and foremost because of the child's great vulnerability. This vulnerability, I would argue, is the reason why crimes against children particularly upset us and provoke a certain protective

---

4. Levinas, *Otherwise Than Being*, 88, emphasis mine.
5. Levinas, *Totality and Infinity*, 199, emphasis mine.

spirit within us. It is also why I fear to turn away from my young child and leave them alone, whether at home or in a public space.

Indeed, this refusal to turn away is for Levinas the very foundation of responsibility for the other. As I explicated in the first section above, the other's face issues a call for attention of a certain kind, attention in a contemplative key, in a posture of wonder and respect. This call takes on a new urgency when the other's face shows its essential finitude (as it always necessarily does, the invisible showing itself in the visibility of finitude). The finitude I meet in the other's face doubles my responsorial task; I am called not only to attention, but to responsibility as well. This responsibility takes on the form first of *staying with* the other, of refusing to turn my back on the other or to get away. It is "an appeal one cannot elude," an assignation from which one "cannot slip away," a call "which cannot be declined."[6] Responsibility for the other is therefore "an obedience [to the other's call] where there is no desertion."[7] Thus the father is often inclined to say to his child the words "I will never leave you." As a father, I must attend *and* I must respond, and I respond first of all by *continuing* to attend, by attending without end. The father in this way finds himself unable, certainly unwilling, to turn away from his child in all their existential vulnerability. He wishes rather to stay with the child as they make their adventure, their passage through the events that will fundamentally shape them and their relation to the world.

As my child's face shows to me their vulnerability and as I take up the parental responsibility of staying with my child, this twofold task of attention and responsibility becomes identificatory for me as father. In some sense, the vulnerability of the child's face chooses the father, who thus becomes "*the chosen or required one*,"[8] the one assigned the task of responsibility for this child's existential need. The assignation of responsibility, and the taking up of such responsibility, accomplishes within the father a new vocation and identity, as he becomes no longer simply an "I-for-myself" but an "I-for-the-other." Levinas says as much: "The for-oneself of identity is now no longer for itself. The identity of the same in the ego comes to it despite itself from the outside, as an election or an inspiration, in the form of the uniqueness of someone assigned. The

6. Levinas, *Otherwise Than Being*, 53.

7. Levinas, *Otherwise Than Being*, 52.

8. Levinas, *Otherwise Than Being*, 56.

subject is for another; its own being turns into for another."⁹ *Affected* by the child's subjection to the evential violence of time and *staying with* the child in a posture of attention and responsibility, I as father become someone new. I am no longer first and foremost the man who enjoys such and such things, but rather the man who has learned—or at least, who is currently learning—how to starve my appetites for enjoyment in order to care for another whose overwhelming need overtakes and greatly diminishes these self-referential appetites. In response to the call of the child's face, with all its neediness, the father arrives with a "Here I am!" and thereby discovers in this response a new "I," the "I-for-the-other."

Responsibility, for Levinas, is thus opposed in some way to the complacency of the self's enjoyment. In Levinas's thought enjoyment marks our fundamental relationship to the world, what we live from and for. We are always following on the heels of some moment of enjoyment and seeking the next one. "We live from 'good soup,'" he says, "air, light, spectacles, work, ideas, sleep, etc., . . . objects of enjoyment, presenting themselves to 'taste,' already adorned, embellished."¹⁰ Important to note here is that the self enjoys in a state of *independence*, and that what it enjoys exists for it on the level of an *object*. In layman's terms, this simply means that enjoyment consists of a self-oriented pleasure experienced in relationship to things that are pleasing to the self. Such enjoyment need not be thought of as morally bankrupt in itself, even for the father; all we are saying here is that the child's face interrupts and relativizes the father's prior baseline mode of enjoyment. The father no longer operates primarily in the mode of being that is enjoyment, which the child's call has muffled and made secondary, but now lives first of all in a new mode of being as affected by the child's face and that we can properly call responsibility. Parental responsibility thus institutes a new and different relationship with enjoyment, one that includes most of all a greater measure of *asceticism*, a diminishment of enjoyment's urgency and importance for me, the father.

The diminishment we speak of here is first passively received before any commitment on the father's part but then also subsequently chosen and enacted with great commitment by the responsible father. My child's call drowns out the noise of my own desires. The child's vulnerability imposes a *quieting* of the appetitive demands that voice within myself for my own enjoyment. Enjoyment thus undergoes a quieting within me, a

9. Levinas, *Otherwise Than Being*, 52.
10. Levinas, *Totality and Infinity*, 110.

diminishment, or a marginalization. The child's face is the light that reveals my own enjoyment to have been rather unimportant all along, and especially now, when the only proper response to the light of the child's face is a breaking off from enjoyment in order to devote my full attention to this face, which calls for my response. As father, I now see that the task of responsibility requires an undivided attention, an attention that is not scattered nor spread thin by the endless flickering of desire here and there and everywhere. My newfound vocation thus prompts me to take up a more ascetical relationship to my own appetites. "To give," then, "to-be-for-another, despite oneself, but in interrupting the for-oneself, is to take the bread out of one's own mouth, to nourish the hunger of another with one's own fasting," "giving the very bread I eat."[11] Of course, the father can choose to eat his own bread. He can go on with his own enjoyment. But he can no longer do so without the pangs of his conscience's cries; to remain complacent in his own enjoyment is now and forevermore to be deaf to his child's call, even to *reject* his child's call.

11. Levinas, *Otherwise Than Being*, 56, 72.

3

Late Modernity's Muting of the Child's Call

"The acceleration of life in general robs the human being of the capacity for contemplation. Thus, those things which only reveal themselves in contemplative lingering remain hidden."

—BYUNG-CHUL HAN[1]

"Our relationships with products tend to be short-lived: rather than hoarding treasured objects, consumers are characterized by a constant dissatisfaction with material goods. This dissatisfaction is what produces the restless pursuit of satisfaction in the form of something new. Consumerism is not so much about having more as it is about having something else; that's why it is not simply buying but shopping that is the heart of consumerism. Buying brings a temporary halt to the restlessness that typifies consumerism. This restlessness—the moving on to shopping for something else, no matter what one has just purchased—sets the spiritual tone for consumerism."

—WILLIAM T. CAVANAUGH[2]

AT THIS POINT WE must also ask what influence the sociohistorical environment has on the manner in which the child's soul appears to us today,

1. Han, *Scent of Time*, 69.
2. Cavanaugh, *Being Consumed*, 35.

and on how the father conceives of the response most proper to the call of the child's soul. In short, we must ask what these phenomena mean in modernity, most especially in our own milieu of late modernity.[3] First, however, I would like to consider one particularly incisive phenomenological critique of modernity, that of Michel Henry, who speaks especially to the role of scientific objectivity in modernity's disintegration. From there, we will move into a more existential consideration of modernity, exploring the psychic conditions the father and child live within in the context of the late modern world and the ways these conditions shape the father–child relationship in important and oftentimes destructive ways. We will consider here in particular some of the barriers to parental responsibility that have arisen in the context of late modernity. In doing so, it will become apparent how certain features of late modern life coalesce to *mute the call of the child's soul* by stripping the father of the *attentional* and *ascetical* capacities that are required for the task of parental responsibility.

3. I am aware that such terms as "modernity," "postmodernity," "late modernity," and so forth have a complicated and contested history. My task here is not to lay out a timeline of the late modern situation—when it began, who or what caused its arrival, how it is distinct from prior epochs, and so on. Nor is my task even to define what this term might mean, which would only be a distracting digression in a book that is, after all, supposed to be about fatherhood. In brief, though, by the term "late modern" I simply mean today's milieu, which I would not characterize as modern or postmodern, but as actually *super*modern, an acceleration of the modern to the point of an unhinged *whizzing*, as Byung-Chul Han would say. In brief, that is, I follow Hartmut Rosa's diagnosis of our contemporary situation as one in which unbridled *acceleration* has become the default mode of being for both society and the individual subject. Of course, much more could be said here about Byung-Chul Han's criticism of Rosa's thesis, and the ways Han situates acceleration as a symptom rather than a cause of humanity's new relationship with time. Han sees time today as unhinged from its previous narratival structure and meaningful end. It now floats freely, "whizzing" around, detached from the connectivities between separate events that were once one of its central features. In this new arrangement, time jumps from one "point-time" to the next, without any possibility for contemplative lingering in the between-times. Acceleration for Han is thus but one of the many effects of time's newfound freedom. On all of this, I agree with Han, even with respect to acceleration's subordination to the "dysynchronicity" of time described above. Still, it seems clear to me that acceleration is the obvious dominant mode of being within today's dysynchronous time. I would also add that this accelerative whizzing is predominantly consumptive in its bearing, driven by a need for increasingly frequent consumption of "content" and product, whether digital or material. We will return to these issues of speed and consumption later. See Rosa, *Social Acceleration*; Han, *Scent of Time*.

There are of course more than a handful of interesting and important critiques of modernity. Within the field of phenomenology, one such critique of modernity that floats to the surface as especially incisive is that of Michel Henry, too little known in Anglophone scholarship to date. For his part, Henry will often label the horizons of modernity as those of the *world*, following the New Testament usage of the word but always with an eye towards the particularly modern iteration of a kind of enclosure within the confines of the atheistic reduction most moderns live under, perhaps even those practicing some religion or other. Higher than this world, though, which Henry never tires of associating with the scientific worldview, is another horizon, which Henry devotes most of his career to delineating: the horizon of *life*. This other horizon is divine in nature and thus marks a theological maneuver of sorts, one in keeping with the descriptions of "Life" in the prologue to John's Gospel. "Life" here refers both to Life (Christ as principle and force of creation) and to life (the many incarnations of Christ's creation, particularly human persons). For Henry, then, there is always a kind of dialectical tension, even opposition, between these horizons, or what we might call forces, of world on the one hand and life on the other. Therefore, he is always situating his critique of the world enclosure in contrastive juxtaposition to an exploration of the life force that creates, sustains, and pulses through everything and everyone.[4]

What Henry means by *life*, however, is in no way straightforward. He often uses other terms in concert with his explorations of life, words like *Arch-intelligibility, auto-affection, transcendental affectivity*, and *flesh*. Leaving aside for now a detailed exposition of these terms, we must note the primary importance of what Henry sometimes calls *Absolute Life*. For Henry, the human person can only find life first within their own internal landscape, a life of the self that exists "in, by, and from" Absolute Life

4. Joseph Rivera says something similar of Henry's thought: "The world does not disappear or dissolve [for Henry] as a useless field of objectivity. Rather, it constitutes the field whereby opposition endlessly confers on the self [as auto-affection, as life] a pressure of difference in the face of the world. I am affected first by myself, and then the world (as horizon) in opposition to myself, which accounts for two fields of display. . . . For Henry, according to the strict logic of phenomenology, a system of manifestation emerges that accounts for two fields of manifestation, or two worlds, really: self-affection versus hetero-affection, or interior self versus exterior world-horizon. . . . The resistance to nihil's pressure is carried out by the self's capacity to hold onto itself by gathering itself within itself, a practice of forceful contradiction of the world-horizon." Rivera, *Phenomenology and the Horizon*, 33, 34, 35.

(that is, Christ).[5] This human life within divine Life is far more certain for Henry than the world, but is distinct from it by its invisibility.[6] Life does not show up for us in visibility, but is rather a feeling of oneself in the experience of oneself, an auto-affection. Within the flesh—much as Merleau-Ponty conceptualized it—within the self's feeling of itself, one finds the capacity for receiving Life, for recognizing the ground of its own life in the Life of God, "vivified by God."[7] Though far from describing the exact same phenomenon, we can tentatively note a rough similarity between what Henry means by *life* and what I have meant here by *soul*. The key distinction would be that Henry's *life* speaks to an experience of oneself, whereas my use of *soul* means to describe one's experience of the other. Both, however, are sensitive to the affective experience of human interiority and to the presence of God as the ground and force of such an affective encounter with either one's own or another's human interiority.

Coming back to Henry, though, we should ask how this experience of life, as he takes up the term, is distinct from the experience of the world. To this question, Henry's critique of modernity is most important. Henry sees modernity as enveloping us within a world that not only closes down the possibility of life's reception but that also actually *defaces* or *profanes* this very life. "With respect to life," he writes, "it [modernity] is an issue of profanation."[8] Modernity thus marks an era in which society has both *stepped on—trampled* would be a better word, perhaps—and *sidelined* life itself. Life is no longer treasured nor important, not even a bygone illusion because it is not even recognized as that which may have once existed as a psychic reality or psychic option. We are no longer aware that this is or was at some point a spiritually legitimate option for anyone; any religiosity must of course have been merely empty gesture, a repressive form of coping with the great epistemic uncertainty we all face, a way of managing or controlling one's own suffering and mortality, perhaps. "If life is [thus] diminished and obscured," says Henry, "if it is no longer the organizing principle of a society and of each one's life within it, the principle of each of its activities, then the time of nihilism has come."[9] This is the heart of Henry's critique of modernity, that it has lost

---

5. Henry, *Incarnation*, 85.

6. Henry, *Incarnation*, 92.

7. Henry here quotes Irenaeus. Henry, *Incarnation*, 133.

8. Henry, *Incarnation*, 219.

9. Henry, *Incarnation*, 219.

life by slowly suffocating life's voice, and that it has done this—wittingly or not—under the regime of scientific certainty, under the thumb of science's drive for objectivity.

Central to Henry's criticism of the modern view of things is what he sees as its idolization of objectivity as a mode of knowledge. He writes, for instance: "*It is a general presupposition of modern knowledge that comes into play*, which takes objectivity as the site of reality, and the knowledge of this reality as the one and only mode of actual knowledge."[10] Two important features of modernity are at work in this statement of Henry's. First, the modern attachment to pure objectivity, to objectivity as the sole "site of reality," closes down any other sites of reality that may exist outside the confines of objecthood. What room is there, then, for any consideration of Marion's "saturated phenomena," those phenomena that seem to paradoxically cloak some invisible excess within their visibility—phenomena like the event, the work of art, the flesh, *the child's face*? Second, there is an existentially felt fallout to the reign of objectivity—namely, again, the nihilistic profanation of life. The human person now sees itself and other persons according to objecthood, as merely objects. But even within this milieu of objectivity, humanity cannot erase its drive for the infinite, and so it will try to produce new conditions for some experience of excess within the walls of its atheistic world. Thus follows all manner of self-abasement: "violence, indignity, infamy, ignominy . . . , prostitution."[11]

We can say with some certainty, then, that the reign of objectivity in the modern world comes to bear on the relationship between the father and the child in ways far too numerous to enumerate here. One particularly salient example, however, is the issue of abortion, surely an act of violence and a destruction of life, we can all admit, whether we fall on the pro-choice or the pro-life side of the aisle.[12] The much-knotted and difficult discussions around when the fetus could be considered a human being, and when, if ever, it is okay to kill this life-form, to "abort" this life springing into being, all seem to miss the very violence of such rhetoric in regards to the unborn child. (Yes, there are exceptions, of course, and yes, sometimes violence is required.) It is remarkable, however, to witness

10. Henry, *Incarnation*, 222.

11. Henry, *Incarnation*, 194.

12. Another example that deserves patient exploration is how scientific objectivity plays out in the medicalization of childhood, particularly with an eye towards the proliferation of behavioral and psychological diagnoses and of their increasingly pharmaceutical treatment.

the manner in which some pro-choice politicians, activists, and yes, even (especially?) scientists deploy the language of scientific objectivity in order to allow the parent to shirk responsibility for this life growing inside the womb. Scientific objectivity, it seems, would render the very most vulnerable among us—the unborn—face-less, soul-less, even life-less, a mere "clump of cells." The responsible father, however, has no thought for measuring the bounds of his responsibility for the life of his child, for his care for the child through all the vulnerabilities the child faces and will face. There is no beginning nor end to the child's call nor to my response as father, precisely because the call and the response speak the voice of some sublime immemorial and unhoped-for, as Jean-Louis Chrétien would put it, some infinity that knows no measures.

It is clear, then, that Henry performs an important and nuanced criticism of the modern age, in his own way. Certainly, too, the issue of objectification comes to bear on the father–child relationship in significant ways, one of which we have explored above with the topic of abortion. Still, I think it would be much more accurate to conceive of modernity's toxins as a complex matrix, with objectivity operating as but one important ingredient among the many at work in said matrix. Perhaps more existentially immediate to the task of parental responsibility is a consideration of the distinctly modern shaping of human desire and its relationship to the human person's experience of their own (and others') limitations and mortality. On these fronts, we find modernity, particularly *late* modernity, presenting ways of life that are perhaps just as toxic as objective reductionism. Indeed, we find forces here that are deadening to the vitality that otherwise brilliantly shines forth in the relationship between father and child, forces that block the father's receptivity to the overfullness that is the child's soul.

To Henry's incisive critiques of modernity, I will add my own, then.[13] Not at all as a corrective to Henry's account but as a way of beginning to round out our understanding of modernity's effects on our most intimate relationships. I will argue here what I have already alluded to above: that late modernity is characterized by, first, a *neurotic relationship with time*, and second, a *disordered appetition*, or what I will call an *appetitional overload*. Both of these, in my view, operate in a mode of burnout,[14] as Byung-Chul Han has labeled it, or a frenzied state of activity and

13. Though I am certainly not the first to voice these particular concerns, and the others who have voiced them before me have done so more poignantly than I could.

14. See Han, *Burnout Society*.

acquisition that perpetuates and intensifies a baseline anxiety verging on panic. This is life in the shitstorm,[15] to borrow another of Han's terms (though applied differently here), life in the chaotic maelstrom of an unrestrained activity and appetite. It knows no self-discipline, no genuine sacrifice for the other except that which is forced on us and to which we reluctantly accommodate. The maelstrom's incessant noise sounds, then, in both the external world and in the interior world. Or rather, it is an external noisiness to which we become so accustomed that it takes up residence interiorly. Perhaps in some sense our acclimation to such an external cacophony requires, or at least begs for, an interior which absorbs and recapitulates the maelstrom in and for oneself. This noise, though, as we will see, drowns out the much gentler sound of the child's call, the sound of the child's soul, and militates against the father's cultivation of the kind of patient attention and readiness for sacrifice that the child's soul calls for.

If we want to adopt Levinas's pejorative use of the term "enjoyment," then we could say that two of the primary manifestations of enjoyment in the modern world are those of *speed* and *consumption*. These speak to the above-mentioned neurotic relationship with time and appetitional overload, respectively. The dominance of speed and consumption in our lives overloads our time and attention to such an extent that we in some sense bathe in a continuous stream of enjoyment, moving without break from one enjoyment to the next, enslaved to the constancy of the accelerative and appetitive thrill. For many of us, there was never some certain point at which we chose to live in such a way; rather, it in some measure *happened to us*, or better, we adapted without even realizing we were doing so. Again, the external maelstrom interiorized itself within each of us, often slowly, bit by bit, until we found ourselves needing it, craving more of the shitstorm. We thus find ourselves living in an environment in which our enculturation develops in us habits that are conducive to enjoyment but injurious of our abilities to attend and to respond with continued attention (to stay with). We are habituated, in other words, to speed and consumption, having lost in some measure the capacity to live otherwise, even though we can remember that we once did indeed live otherwise, before the maelstrom spread within our person like some kind of sickness and came over time to transform us into creatures with an altogether different mode of being in the world. In this mode of being,

15. See Han, *In the Swarm*.

speed measures both the maximal volume of activity that the modern person undertakes as well as the maximal pace at which the modern person performs said activity. Productivity and efficiency are the key indicators of success here. And for its part, *consumption* is likewise a measure of success in a special way for modern persons, but in this case it is a matter of the acquisition and possession of goods, whether material or immaterial. Quantity and quality of goods figure here as marks of status, both to oneself and to others.

This sickness of the self, wrought by the interiorization of the shitstorm, never seems to reign entirely uncontended, however. The good dies hard, it would seem. In short, we can still hear the call of the other's soul even in the cacophonous maelstrom of enjoyment in which we live. The manifestations of ethical injunctions in our lives still speak to us in such a way, with a certain potency, that they often succeed even in today's unfavorable conditions at interrupting the flow of enjoyment. Indeed, the call to intersubjective attention and responsibility appears to be one of the few remaining forces that can contend with the maelstrom's sheer power. Still, as parents in the late modern world, we experience the call of the child's soul and our immersion in the maelstrom as cross-pressured, borrowing Charles Taylor's term here. The father hears the call not as a clear voice in the quiet, but as calling out at variable decibels from among all the din of late modern life. It is not a call out in the open, so to speak, but a call piercing through a dense fog. The sociocultural conditions of late modernity work together to mute the child's call, and so the father—in a special way today—finds he must perform a kenotic movement, emptying himself of late modernity's many temptations to speed and consumption, in order to attend and respond to his child faithfully. He has to find some way to quiet the noise, to cultivate enough quiet within himself to hear the call of the child's soul. But in our day he is working against considerable odds in this effort, which requires what we might think of as a certain spiritual maturity and thus a mode of being in the world that is distinct from modernity's vain insatiability, even if this spiritual maturity is always necessarily and inevitably intermingled with the maelstrom that is the milieu in which the father lives and that has in some measure inscribed itself in his very person.

We have elaborated in some detail on the place of attention and asceticism in the task of parental responsibility. What I want to say now is that late modernity's maelstrom negates these, and more specifically, that *speed wears down our attentional capacities*, on the one hand, and that *(hyper)consumption erodes our ascetical abilities*, on the other. First, let us consider the issue of speed as it relates to the attention required for the parental vocation. It is no secret that we live in an age that idolizes speed. We are immersed in an era that wants everything as quick as humanly possible, whether in the form of food, a book ordered online, or an email reply. Moreover, in America especially, and particularly for those wishing to be upwardly mobile, our "work lives" are defined by an always insatiable need for greater speed, for increased efficiency and productivity. (Note, for instance, that Artificial Intelligence seems to be taking off most forcefully in the workplace, where it is marketed as a tool for quicker and easier results, thus freeing up more time for, well, more work.)

For all its benefits—and there are many, to be sure!—the undeniable problem with speed is that it bars the necessary space and silence for reflection. It fills our lives with noise, to come back to our earlier metaphor. By barring the kind of stillness conducive to a certain attention that is placid in quality, speed breaks down the existential depth and the contemplative presence that help so much to hear the call of the child's face, the call of the child's soul. As a father, too much speed in my life spreads my attentional energies thin, so while I might be doing all the things a responsible father is supposed to do—going to my child's sporting events, teaching my child how to calm themselves down when they are emotionally elevated, tucking my child back into bed when they wake up from a nightmare, etc.—it may be the case that I am performing these tasks with only the most feeble and bare minimum of attention required. In short, I can do all the right things as a father without ever really noticing my child's soul which speaks to me in their eyes, or without ever appreciating this child's face with that utmost wonder and respect it deserves. Speed has this way, it turns out, of sapping our attentional strength such that we live in large part on a kind of attentional autopilot, so to speak, always on to the next item.

Consumption as a mode of being then further undercuts the kinds of capabilities the child's soul calls for. More to the point, the hyper-consumption to which we are all accustomed in the late modern West has a deteriorating effect on the father's ascetical capacities. In fact, consumption invades and thus further corrupts our already-depleted attention. It does so by slowly seducing us into a now-customary *consumptive mode of attention*. This form of attention is entirely alien to that more patient and contemplative type of which we have spoken so much in these pages. It is a greedy and consuming attention, a fixation always on the next fix, as it were. It leaves us always on the hunt for some novelty to enjoy, some news item or Twitter trend, a development in our favorite sports league or a new episode of our favorite show on Netflix, an exciting career opportunity or our next tropical vacation. In this mode of being, this manner of existence in the maelstrom, we find ourselves living always for the next titillation. Indeed, we find ourselves in need of that next auto-erotic fix, addicted to our enjoyment, turned in on ourselves and bathing in our own desire. Levinas is most incisive in his consideration of this kind of enjoyment:

> Here lies the permanent truth of hedonist moralities: to not seek behind the satisfaction of need, an order relative to which alone satisfaction would acquire a value; to take satisfaction, which is the very meaning of pleasure, as a term. . . . In enjoyment, I am absolutely for myself. Egoist without reference to the Other. . . . Not against the Other, not "as for me . . ."—but entirely deaf to the Other, outside of all communication and all refusal to communicate—without ears, like a hungry stomach.[16]

This, indeed, is precisely what I mean when I talk about *the consumptive mode of attention*. Existing in its whirlpool, the father knows not how to break free from his appetitive overload. His incapacity to hem in all the noise of his desires, to cultivate appetitive quiet in his interior life, spreads his attention thin all the more, again leaving him with only the feeblest of attention to offer his child. He learns to be responsive to his child's need in a rather inattentive sort of way, without stilling himself for the fuller task of kneeling down and noticing the child's soul, and then responding to it with the proper wonder and respect, which can only come from a close proximity to the sacredness of the child's face, from taking the care to envisage the surplus in the child's eyes.

For Levinas it would seem that enjoyment has a necessarily negative moral status. But we should ask: Does the experience of enjoyment qua enjoyment always, in every case, feature this deafness to the other's call, or should we speak rather of this deafness as a perversion of a more original enjoyment that is morally positive, or at least neutral? What should we make, for instance, of the experience of enjoying the other, or even of enjoying the task of sacrifice for the other, enjoying the vocation of responsibility? The responsible father knows well the enjoyment that can well up from an act of patient attention with his child, or of meeting his child's need, which may sometimes arrive for the father as an experience

16. Levinas, *Totality and Infinity*, 134.

of sublime communion with his child. Enjoyment in itself does not seem to be the problem, then, but rather an overindulgent enjoyment that is wholly self-absorbed and self-interested. It is this kind of enjoyment, a *perversion* of enjoyment, we could say, that endangers the father–child relationship, or at the very least seriously stunts the father's hearing of the child's call and his readiness for response. What fathers today most lack is the spiritual skillset of attention and asceticism that would equip them to be better able to *relativize* their own enjoyment so as to be more available and responsible for their children. Speed and consumption, however, late modernity's capital forms of enjoyment, tend to spoil the father's (good and original) appetitive nature as geared towards enjoyment on another level, that is, as enjoyment *of the other* and of life *for the other*.

In the end, it might be better to speak of this enjoyment-on-another-level not as *enjoyment*, which rightly has all the Levinasian connotations of self-absorption and self-interest, but instead as a manifestation of *joy*. This joy is that spiritual and sacrificial enjoyment beyond enjoyment, or enjoyment beyond self-enjoyment, and is borne of a vocation for attention and responsibility. The life founded on these is in large measure one that has a joyous affective hue. In this mode of being, the father delights in his child, in the environment of the home, and in all the small (and sometimes big) ways he gets to provide care for his child. Pope Francis's *Amoris Laetitia* is particularly illuminating on this point:

> "Through their union in love, the couple experiences the beauty of fatherhood and motherhood, and shares plans, trials, expectations and concerns; they learn care for one another and mutual forgiveness. In this love, they celebrate their happy moments and support each other in the difficult passages of their life together. . . . The beauty of this mutual, gratuitous gift, the joy which comes from a life that is born and the loving care of all family members—from toddlers to seniors—are just a few of the fruits which make the response to the vocation of the family unique and irreplaceable," both for the Church and for society as a whole.[17]

We see here an image of family life that is saturated with the kind of joy that can only come from an immersion in the many textures of familial responsibility, sharing "plans, trials, expectations and concerns," learning "care for one another and mutual forgiveness." This is no late modern's individualistic dream we are talking about here. In fact, to put

---

17. Francis, *Amoris Laetitia*, §88. Francis is quoting *Relatio Finalis*, §§49–50.

the matter bluntly, we see that late modernity, with all its cult of objectivity and technicization and all its worship of speed and consumption, has slowly and steadily worked to exterminate precisely this kind of life together, this manner of living for the other. It is no mystery why we notice so many young people in my generation repulsed by the idea of settling down with a spouse and starting a family. There is too much work involved in this way of life, too much inconvenience, too much sacrifice of my own self-enjoyment, too much compromise on all my dreams and aspirations for myself.

And yet we have to ask: what spiritual maturity and what fullness of joy are lost in such an aversion to a life of responsibility for others? The answer, it seems, is precisely the capacity for patient and sustained attention and for thoroughgoing responsibility for others, not to mention the opportunity for a life with and for others that is saturated with a joy beyond self-enjoyment. As a culture, therefore, our call today is to cultivate within ourselves and within our homes a way of living otherwise than the way of the maelstrom, a manner of existence that bears those now-strange fruits of patient contemplation and self-restraint. Only thus can we recover a fuller experience of what it means to give oneself to and for the child and to find in this self-gift a communion with the child that far surpasses any of the enjoyments of modernity's maelstrom. What we need, in short, is a fresh expression of what one might call a prayerful life, or a prayerful mode of living. If, as a society, we want to attend to the souls of children as they deserve, we need to open ourselves again to the experience of astonishment, to remember what it is like to live unshielded, available for all the moments when wonder begs to strike. It is a prayerful patience down on one's knees, a contemplation that alone quiets all the internal and external noise enough for us to see the saturation beyond saturation that is the child and their soul, pure gift.

4

The Unthinkable Sacrifice

"To attain this ability to be present supposes the opposite of stiffness and withdrawal: a flexibility, a pliability, a letting go, and, to put it bluntly, an exposure and a nakedness, such that what comes to meet us has permission to do so without detours, and without having to cross multiple lines of fortification. What could be more nude and receptive than an attentive, collected face?"

—JEAN-LOUIS CHRÉTIEN[1]

"Spirit becomes mine only when something in me shatters and loses itself as gift."

—JEAN-LOUIS CHRÉTIEN[2]

FOR ALL THE JOY the father can find in his child, we should not diminish the fact that the father's responsibility is also a great burden to carry, and indeed that the burden of responsibility is so great as to often seem overwhelming. Faced with all the exorbitant need calling from the child's face, the father confronts both his own limitations and his capacity for violence. It would not be hyperbolic, at least in the case of the *young* child, to speak of an onslaught of overwhelming need that issues from

1. Chrétien, *Ten Meditations*, 55.
2. Chrétien, *The Call and the Response*, 44.

the child's face. Levinas will speak, for instance, of responsibility as an experience of "inexhaustible obligations,"[3] and to this I would add how as father I am always "back on my heels" before I even have the chance to respond to my child's call, that the child's face leaves me "surprised, taken aback, slapped awake," and facing an overwhelming array of demands I could never possibly oblige in full. Though I respond with my "Here I am," I find that "in approaching the other [in our case, the child] I am *always late for the meeting*."[4] I arrive and patiently attend, but when I arrive, I discover a tremendous vulnerability that I am not prepared for and that in truth outstrips all my preparation and all my readiness to respond. My daughter's need is greater than what I can think, and so my response is in some measure unplannable since I cannot think the need except within the immediacy of the concrete situation in which it expresses itself directly before my eyes. But when it appears in the concrete situation, I find I have no plan, no sure self-guidance that I could have pre-conceived. I am operating on the fly, grasping for resources somewhere deep in my own reserves ("where is that damn thing?"), unsure how to respond to such a surplus of need and fumbling my way through in my attempt to respond.

There is therefore an inevitable inadequacy to the father's response to his child's need. The child in all their soul-fullness and all their vulnerability deserves, in some sense, a fullness of response and a sureness that the father ultimately cannot offer them. As a father, I see myself as exposed in this moment of inadequacy, matching my child's vulnerability with my own, embarrassed at myself for the lack of sureness in my response (even if I feign it), realizing with new immediacy my inability to offer my child the fullness of response that is beyond what I can think. And yet I offer my own vulnerability to my child as a gift of love. I go to that place in which my reserves run low, and I find myself in an embarrassing search for resources, and I do this because my child's call reaches my ears and because I want to respond with the utmost respect and wonder. This moment thus brings together my daughter's vulnerability with my own, and in this act of mutual self-exposure we share in the "shakenness" of our humanity, to borrow a term from Jan Patočka. There is therefore a communion here in our woundedness, where the father finds the only adequate response to the child's vulnerability is to exhaust his

---

3. Robbins, *Is It Righteous to Be?*, 112.
4. Levinas, *Otherwise Than Being*, 150, emphasis mine.

efforts at adequacy and thereby show his own vulnerability. This, again, is a self-offering, the most precious and important gift perhaps that a father can offer his child.

This intimacy of two vulnerabilities is by turns glorious and terrifying, though. Where there is the greatest self-exposure, there is the greatest fear of the trespass and most especially of violence. Only the utmost trust can endure such intimacy. And in this intimacy, the father experiences more than ever the supremely important call to protect the child's soul in all its vulnerability, to protect the child's soul even from himself. Only within such intimacy can the child's soul be loved, and only in such intimacy can the child's soul be murdered. The child's self-exposure, their soul-in-vulnerability, is a holy ground in which the father recognizes he must remove his shoes but finds himself yet kicking up dust. Here he knows his own violence and sees it in his own footsteps. (And best not to imagine the possibility of the violence of others—which may well be a great deal more dangerous than his own—trespassing on such sacred terrain.) In this mutual exposure between father and child, the father experiences the unsurpassable impossibility of violence, and yet finds himself still frightened by its possibility. Again, he searches in vain for a sureness to his response; how can he know for sure this violence is unsurpassably impossible; moreover, how can he know for sure others will not trespass where they ought not? In the moment of most intimate exposure, the interdiction resounds deep within the father's psyche, deep down to his very bones: "Thou shalt not kill." Here he knows a sacred terror following from and equal to the preciousness of the child's soul, a terror that shakes him even more violently than the shakenness that is constitutive of his human finitude.

We are now entering the territory, then, of that most disturbing of biblical stories, the Akedah, or the binding of Isaac, an image of what I will call *the unthinkable sacrifice*. If we look at the text of the Akedah closely, we will notice that God provides Abraham with no reason for asking him to sacrifice his beloved son, Isaac. There is simply the command, and then the response:

> After these things God tested Abraham, and said to him, "Abraham!" And he said, "Here am I." He said, "Take your son, your only begotten son Isaac, whom you love, and go to the land of Mori'ah, and offer him there as a burnt offering upon one of the mountains of which I shall tell you." So Abraham rose early in the morning, saddled his donkey, and took two of his young

men with him, and his son Isaac; and he cut the wood for the
burnt offering, and arose and went to the place of which God
had told him. (Gen 22:1–3)

In other words, this is for Abraham a sacrifice for nothing, by which I
mean a sacrifice given as a measure of his commitment to love nothing
but God, a sacrifice to *have* nothing as a test of his love of God. It is a
question of possessiveness. Abraham is ready to do the unthinkable to
Isaac and so to *lose* his beloved. In this moment of testing, he cannot *have*
his son; that is, he cannot hold onto him tightly, so to speak. Ironically
enough, Isaac here is pure gift, the furthest thing from property or possession. Even the joy beyond enjoyment of the father–child relationship
is not something the father can claim possession of. Abraham is ready
to make the sacrifice no father—certainly not I!—can bring himself to
make, to have such a singular devotion as to be willing to completely
deface himself, to do the unthinkable. He is prepared to deface himself
without any hope for recovery (how could a father ever recover from this,
both within himself and among his community?). The intimate terror
of which we spoke earlier visits Abraham in this moment, the intimate
exposure of his child's face. He is about to perform an irreversible trauma
that will not only exterminate the life of his son but ruin his own life as
well. The thought of his son's face will forever after torture him. On the
mountaintop, with his boy tied up and laid on the firewood, with his
knife in hand, Abraham is the epitome of the holy fool. And who would
want to be in his position? Who would want to be the holy fool?

A further example: Andrei Tarkovsky's *The Sacrifice* shows us another father–son relationship pushed to the edge of an unthinkable sacrifice. In the movie, the protagonist, Alexander, is the father of Tommy, a
young boy who cannot be more than five years of age and who is apparently mute. Alexander and the rest of the family are fond of calling the
young boy by the moniker "Little Man." Early in the film, we see images
of an affectionate bond between the two. Alexander and Little Man work
together to lift and replant a dead tree; the boy sits in his father's lap as
they rest against a tree in the woods; at moments the two hold hands
as they walk along the path. These images of affection are interrupted,
however, by the sounds of war planes above and explosions far off. We
see wine glasses shaking on a pewter tray, a glass milk jug topple off a
shelf and shatter on the floor below, a shot of an alleyway strewn with

half-burnt papers, broken chairs, discarded clothes, and an overturned car. We hear talk of World War III and a nuclear holocaust.

As the movie slowly wends its way through the family's torturous realizations, coming on in waves, of what is to come, Alexander grows more and more mute, like his boy, and thinks more and more of performing some sacrifice to save his family, Little Man most especially. The postman then visits Alexander privately to inform him that if he wants "all of this to be over and done with," then he must "lie with Maria," one of the family maids and apparently a witch. The postman further instructs Alexander: "It's very simple. She lives alone. *And if you only wish for one thing at that moment*: That all this will be over, then it will be!" And so Alexander goes and does precisely this. He visits the woman and makes his request, the two of them levitating while making love.

But Alexander then doubles down on his sacrifice with another sacrifice, this one much more public: he returns home while his family members are all away, stacks up the chairs and curtains on top of the dining room table, lights a match, and sets his family home ablaze. In the film's climactic sequence, we watch as the family returns to find the house completely engulfed in flame, the fire's punishing flames rising up to the sky, and Alexander standing there before the house like a mute idiot. Alexander fumbles around the field like a madman, his family shouting after him, before he enters the back of an ambulance and is taken away. The film then ends with a scene of Little Man carrying a bucket of water to the dead tree that he and his father resurrected and replanted, whereupon he watches the ambulance drive away with his father in tow. He waters the dead tree and lies down at its base. Lying at the foot of the tree, staring up at the sky, the mute boy at last finds his voice and speaks: "In the beginning was the Word. . . . Why is that, Papa?"

As with Abraham, Alexander's sacrifice represents an act of total self-defacement, though Alexander actually carries through with the act. There can be no recovery for Alexander after this; he will always be the lunatic, the man who burned down his own family home. Even if he in some sense recovers—let us say, he spends some time in a psychiatric ward and "gets better"—still he cannot erase the fact of his act and the fact that it comprises part of his life story, and a major part at that, a part that alters his life considerably, and in some sense destroys his life. Will he ever be allowed to reside with his son again, for instance? Will be able to re-establish his marital bond and the mutual trust required therein? How will he manage to fold back into the community? The answers to these questions are unclear, even undecidable, which is precisely what makes this an *unthinkable* sacrifice, a sacrifice beyond what Alexander can think, beyond what he can pre-meditate. He knows not the extent of the consequences and in fact could not possibly know what wake will follow from this act. What he *can* think is that it will irreparably harm the life he knows and deface through-and-through his previously established identity. He will lose in some sense his relationship with his son, his marriage will be jeopardized if not ruined. He will lose his career as a lecturer and any measure of respect he previously knew with his colleagues and with the community in which he lives. Driven away in the back of an ambulance, we can surmise that he will now either live in a psychiatric ward or a prison, or perhaps both. His life as he knew it is over. Like Abraham, in this moment he is the epitome of the holy fool, having given over every vestige of egological presentation to the fires of his sacrificial act.

Alexander's sacrifice not only defaces his own sense of self, though, but also betrays that which he holds most dear, paradoxically as an act of love for that which he holds most dear. This act is one in which he is choosing to abandon his wife and son, to burn their life together down to the ground, and to leave them to fend for themselves, now without a home or an income provider. He not only loses his beloved, but even *hurts* his beloved. This is a sacrifice that profanes the intimate trust of the father–child relationship, betraying the communion that holds Alexander and Little Man together in their mutual self-exposure. But Alexander's betrayal of what he holds most dear, his little boy, is at another level a sacrifice that is so pure in love for what it holds most dear that it is willing to lose what it holds most dear for the sake of what it holds most dear. Only after an act so pure in love does Little Man's voice spring forth. From this strange sacrifice that disfigures everything for Alexander—his sense of self, his relationships, his whole life—comes new life. Love here begets life. More precisely, love at its very ugliest brings into being something beautiful and unexpected. The boy watches his father leave him, and then his voice pours forth under the resurrected tree. The father has accomplished a truly Christic act, life bubbling up from the remains of his death to self.

There is something reminiscent here, as in the case of Abraham, of what Jean-Yves Lacoste has called "the minimal man." The minimal man, for Lacoste, is the one who has chosen "voluntary poverty," and "whoever desires poverty . . . wants nothing other than to accede to the truth of his being." "We all live this knowledge" of our fundamental ontological poverty, he goes on, "if we accept that our death challenges our every relation to possession."[5] Simply put, the minimal man lives in the truth that he owns nothing, and for the father living in such a frame, he owns not even his relationship with his child. The child escapes his possession, dear as this beloved one is to him. The minimal man is able to accept and advene to, borrowing again Romano's term, this failure of possession that is part and parcel of his human finitude. Lacoste continues,

> Those who liturgically face the Absolute [i.e., those who live in relationship to God] neither have anything nor can take possession of anything. Nothing they could have in their possession contributes to the expression of their identity, and they are offered nothing they could take possession of. There is no question of lording over things; man is laid bare, and because his act of presence does nothing but put him at the mercy of gifts he can only patiently wait for, it must be said that he is—definitively—poor.[6]

The minimal father, then, would be the one who lets the brilliance of the child's face, the child's soul, shine forth without any interference on his part, without any efforts to bind this brilliant soul to himself, to hold onto it possessively, to claim it as his own or to resist any movements it may make away from him. We are speaking here of a non-possessive sense of attention and responsibility, what we might more aptly and simply call love.

The minimal father is also ready to accept that all the egological aspects of his fatherhood are fleeting, that his fatherhood is indeed not about him nor about any attributes he possesses. He is laid bare, as Lacoste says, choosing to expose his own existential nakedness, having nothing to give his child but his own poverty, his own exposure. Here in this exposure, though, he experiences a communion with his child that is more primordial than any egological construction could ever hope to be, and therein he finds a truer self, the vocational self, the self given over for another. Kenosis, it turns out, is the key to a truer self underneath the egological self, a self that by its non-possessive love draws out the life of another, allows this other the space to emerge, now shining in the light of the wonder and respect with which I envisage this other. The minimal father is like John the Baptist, who says of Jesus, "He must increase, but I

5. Lacoste, *Experience and the Absolute*, 172–74.
6. Lacoste, *Experience and the Absolute*, 174.

must decrease" (John 3:30 ESV). He draws himself back, that is, he draws back his self-presentation, his need to *be something* in this face-to-face encounter with his child, makes himself small so as to let his child take the stage. Again, the minimal father recognizes that this face-to-face encounter with his child is not about him. He is not here to celebrate himself and his parental identity, but to envisage his child, to attend patiently to the child's face. In this moment, he is not about himself, but about his child. This kenotic movement, too, is a sacrifice borne of loving responsibility and is possible only by a certain spiritual maturity consistent with the kind of attentional and ascetical capacities we spoke of earlier.

We still need, however, to provide a fuller description of those not-so-serene phenomena that sometimes visit even the spiritually mature father and that confront him with the thought of the sort of unthinkable sacrifice we saw with Abraham and Alexander. We should be grateful that as parents it is very unlikely we will be called upon to make the kind of ruinous sacrifice that Alexander makes and that Abraham comes to the brink of. In short, these two fathers perform a sacrifice that most of us gratefully do not *have to* perform, and that most of us in truth *could not* perform. But what of those unsettling psychic phenomena in which the thought of an unthinkable violence against our children visits us against our wills? What of those fearsome images of some irreparable harm, some trauma, befalling our children, those unwelcome cogitations that the psychotherapeutic establishment calls "intrusive thoughts" and that are known to visit the new mother (and sometimes, it must be said, as in my own case, the new father)? In the face of such phenomena, so common for parents, particularly parents of young children, we must admit the reality of visceral fears that prey upon the parent as if from nowhere and that disturb the psychic tranquility of those early years of parenthood which are marked by the most trusting and affectionate intimacy. The father in this case is forced, as it were, to think the unthinkable, though he wishes desperately that the thought of the unthinkable would evacuate his mind, and that it would do so fast. Like Abraham and Alexander, the father comes face-to-face with the possibility of some major trauma inflicted on his child, the prospect of his child undergoing some evential violence that seems almost too much to bear for the father, even the death of his child, which indeed can only ever be too much to bear for the father. He finds himself against his will thinking the unthinkable sacrifice, tortured by the thought's unwelcome visitation.

Of course, it is one thing to be the agent of such an unthinkable sacrifice, to deliberately inflict some harm on the child or on one's relationship with the child. It is quite another to be a passive victim, in a sense, of intrusive thoughts about some horror or violence visiting one's child, some horror or violence that one would never deliberately inflict upon their child. These are obviously not at all the same things. And yet there is some relationship, some similarity, between the sacrifice (willingly) performed and the sacrifice (unwillingly) imagined. In fact, I would argue that both are forms of sacrifice in that they entail a surrender of control over the child's life (and death) as well as a facing up to the worst imaginable scenarios befalling the child and/or the parent-child relationship. Both are experiences at the extreme threshold between what the parent can tolerate and what the parent cannot tolerate regarding their child. Each confronts the parent with the tremendous and terrifying challenge of making them intimate with the most profound anguish, a sacrifice beyond what they can bear.

The *unthinkable* here speaks to the unbearable pain that pierces the parent—an unthinkable pain, a pain that is too visceral to think, too overwhelming for language. Moreover, it is a pain the responsible parent would *not want* to think. The *unthinkable* means the untouchable, the defiling, anathema. It is whatever the parent least wants to face, some prospect regarding one's child that one cannot bear to think about. And the *unthinkable* here speaks also to the undecidability of the trauma's consequences; the parent cannot visit the abyss of profound loss beforehand, cannot try it out and see what it's like ahead of time; rather, the parent hurtles or falls headlong into it and only then experiences the depths of panic and despair. But even before such a trauma, at just the thought of it, one knows well the terror of the sharp ledge and the haunt of the possible irreversible fall into the abyss. What the parent cannot know ahead of time is what it will really be like to live in the abyss, to go on living after the child's trauma, how one will manage to cope and to scrape some kind of life together in the wake of this evential violence.

What I mean to describe here by speaking of "thinking the unthinkable sacrifice" could be described as an experience of *terror*, particularly the terror that arrives for the father with the onset of intrusive thoughts around some major trauma befalling his child. We can think of this terror as in some sense taking up residence within the father, or as *haunting* him. Romano provides a nice exposition of terror as I mean it here:

In considering the phenomenon of terror, we can attempt to bring to light this alteration of passibility by analyzing how the impossibility of any response to a traumatizing event entails a profound modification of our relation to this event, which suddenly frees itself from the limits of this singular experience and invades our whole adventure through its repetition in memory or dreams and, impossible to assimilate, becomes a genuine "foreign body," as Freud put it so well. . . . If selfhood is indeed the capacity-to-face what happens to us, so as to appropriate it as such, in terror by contrast *there is no longer any "facing"*: an *advenant* is delivered without reserve to the anonymous and faceless otherness of the terrifying, which overruns him entirely, chills him to the bones, transfixes him, and so on.[7]

Romano here considers terror *resulting from* trauma, whereas I am speaking about terror *at the prospect of* trauma. But the phenomenological similarities between the two types of relation with trauma obtain for our purposes a common phenomenal description, such that what Romano describes is precisely what I mean here, that is, a relentless and repetitive invasion of a foreign body that can only be described as the terror of the unthinkable.

What the father is dealing with here is the haunting intrusion of the unthinkable thought, which makes him shudder and which takes him over. What he experiences in this moment—often carried on in a torturous sequence of moments, hours, days, weeks, even months or years—is a visceral confrontation with an unreal threat to his child that nonetheless visits him as if it were impending and sends shockwaves, as it were, through both his psyche and body. He is in a sense possessed, unable to reach his own store of resources for accommodating to the (in this case psychic) evential violences he undergoes, resources that the terror seems to bury underground, completely unavailable and useless. The unthinkable thought visits the father and obtains an intimacy he would much rather shirk but that has taken him over, leaving him no opportunity for escape. Romano, again, writes, "the terrifying declares itself to us in a *proximity without distance* that abolishes any possibility of flight and leaves us paralyzed, numbed, and defenseless. . . . [I]t is an *obsessive mode of enveloping*."[8]

7. Romano, *Event and World*, 109.
8. Romano, *Event and World*, 109.

We turn now to another filmic example that enlivens the terror of which we are speaking. The movie in question is Jordan Peele's 2017 horror film, *Get Out*. In the film Chris, a young black man, and his girlfriend Rose, a young white woman, visit Rose's family at their immaculate home in upstate New York. Gradually, Rose's family and friends start to show what some have called a kind of "benevolent racism." As Chris and Rose drive up to the house, Chris notices an African-American groundskeeper tending the front lawn. Rose's father, Dean, a well-to-do neurosurgeon, greets Chris at the door with a "my man" and seems bent on highlighting to Chris his appreciation of Barack Obama and Jesse Owens. Chris later meets the family's African-American maid, whose catatonic demeanor strikes him as rather unnatural. At dinner, Rose's younger brother Jeremy, apparently drunk, asks Chris if he likes MMA fighting or if he ever got into any "street fights" growing up. He then follows up, now whispering, his tone more intense, more charged, a somewhat demented smile creeping out from under his lips: "'Cause with your frame and genetic makeup, if you really pushed your body, and I mean really trained, you know, no pussyfooting around, you'd be a *fucking* beast." Missy then has to call Jeremy off as he prepares to put Chris in a headlock at the dinner table.

On their first evening at the family house, we also learn that Rose's mother, Missy, is a hypnotist when she and Dean offer to help Chris quit his smoking addiction through hypnotherapy. At night, unable to sleep and craving a smoke, Chris finds Missy in a sitting room, where she is apparently sipping a cup of tea. He sits down across from her, and as they start to talk, Missy introduces the topic of hypnotism and begins gently scraping her spoon along the wall of her teacup, a gentle and lulling noise coming from the spoon's contact with the cup. Chris starts to wonder if Missy has already begun hypnotizing him as she asks him questions about his mother's death. The spoon now in a constant, gentle scraping rotation along the cup's wall, again and again, Chris starts to answer Missy's questions, tearfully narrating how on the night of his mother's death, still a young boy, he sat at home by himself watching TV, wondering why his mother was not home yet, but doing nothing, taking no action. "You're so scared," Missy says to him. "You think it was your fault." Sitting in his chair across from Missy, Chris realizes aloud that he can no longer move. Missy confirms this: "You can't move. You're paralyzed. Just like that day when you did nothing. *You did nothing.*" A few moments of silence pass, then Missy interjects in a low voice: "Now . . . sink into the floor." We then see Chris falling slowly through a black, outer-space-like atmosphere, falling slowly away from a screen-like image of Missy. From this screen high above him, so resembling the TV screen he watched as a young boy during his mother's dying moments, up above this black space he now floats in, Missy calmly (and creepily) says to him: "Now you're in the sunken place."

The following day, Dean and Missy host a party for their friends, an eclectic cast of characters, mostly white, who make all sorts of strange and ignorant racial comments to Chris and Rose. These friends want to know if Chris has any golf talent like Tiger Woods, if the sex is better with a black man, what Chris's opinions are on the cultural fashionability of blackness, etc., etc. From afar, Chris spots another younger black man at the party and approaches him. "Good to see another brother around here," he says to him. But Chris is taken aback when the man, who introduces himself as Logan, shows the same kind of catatonic demeanor as the family maid had earlier in the movie. When Chris later snaps a photograph of Logan from his phone, the camera accidentally flashes, and Logan's eyes suddenly become wide and wet with oncoming tears, a drop of blood trickling from his nose, too. Mouth trembling, he tells Chris to "get out." Then rising to a scream, and now charging Chris, Logan continues, grabbing Chris by the shirt: "Get out! Get out of here! Get the fuck out of here!" From this point, Chris discovers, with the help of his friend back home, who is doing some research for him and connecting the dots, that this Logan is actually a mutual friend of theirs whom Chris had until then not recognized, a man from Brooklyn named Andre whom the police had reported as missing. After Logan has a hypnosis session with Missy, though, he is back to his catatonic state, apologizing to Chris and the other guests for his behavior and dismissing himself from the party.

Chris and Rose then venture down to the lake behind the house. Meanwhile, we see Dean conducting a game of silent bingo in the backyard for his guests, a framed photo of Chris sitting on a pedestal next to him, Chris apparently being the prize for the game of bingo. Gradually we discover that Dean and Missy, together with their children, are running a not-so-benevolent enterprise in which they offer interested clients a neurological transplant that allows them to take up residence, as it were, in the bodies of the black men and women whom Rose and Jeremy lure to their family's estate. The consciousnesses of these black men and women, all hypnotized by Missy, remain in "the sunken place." They become entirely passive onlookers viewing reality from afar, just as Chris had looked up—as through a TV screen—at the real scene of

Missy speaking to him, looked on at reality from deep down in the darks of the sunken place, unable to climb back up into reality. The beneficiary transplantee, on the other hand, now gets to benefit from whatever they had desired in that particular black person's physicality, perhaps a better golf swing, better sex, a certain fashionability, and so on.

The father's terror at the thought of the unthinkable befalling his child, I want to say, is in some measure akin to the scenario played out in Peele's unsettling film. As with Chris, it is the thought of a serious trauma that enacts a kind of hypnosis for the father. In Chris's case, this is the thought of his mother's death, and of his failure to respond, his failure to call 9-1-1 as the hours dragged on and his mother never came home. For the father, it is the thought of his child undergoing some unspeakable trauma, the thought of which is its own kind of psychic trauma. In both cases, the thought of the unthinkable, of that which one desperately wishes not to think, exercises a kind of hypnosis, a falling through the floor, as it were, and falling away from reality. The father in this case becomes overtaken by a terror that erupts from some unreal prospect, some prospect that in reality he need not worry about, but that against his will worries him still, more than worries him, really, terrorizes him. This thought's visitation is an unwelcome intrusion, taking up residence within oneself and thereby taking the reins, so to speak, much as Dean and Missy's hypothetical client would come to take the reins of a young black man like Chris. All the while, the father, like Chris, is pushed down into a "sunken place," watching on, unable to access the more grounded and real mode of being to which he was previously accustomed and to which he longs to return, the mode of being that was free from terror's inscription within himself. The sight of it, of reality, far off, too far to reach, teases the father and makes his passive torment all the worse. He only wants to again exist free from the terror of the unthinkable thought, in a mode of being that is marked by a relative peace he has seemingly lost. The terror of the unspeakable haunts the father, steals any tranquility he has known, and dislodges him from his groundedness in the real world, drops him down against his will into an unreal world, the world of the most torturous prospect, of the worst imaginable scenario, the scenario that in all reality may never actually arrive. (So why torture oneself with such thoughts, we might ask. But the problem is, the father in this case does not choose to, indeed, he wishes he could wish the thoughts away, but his wishes obtain no escape for him.)

How is the father, then, to manage the phenomenon of terror, to adapt himself to the most undesirable "mental events" that visit him? How can he acclimate himself to these new and unexpected thoughts that seem to be entirely out of his control? What must he do to advene to the torturous prospect, or must he advene to it all? Should he not rather respond to the prospect with a firm rejection, or will such efforts at resistance only tighten the spring of these thoughts, visiting him now with a redoubled vengeance?

Some of us, as parents, it seems, irrespective of any decision on our part, must learn to face the terror of the unthinkable thought, must learn to live under these terrorizing thoughts in a position of total exposure. I suspect more parents than not are neurotic in this way in their relationship with their child. I do not mean this pejoratively, for what it is worth, for parental neurosis is itself its own kind of attestation of love. In other words, I would hazard that what I am speaking of here—the distinctly parental neurosis of intrusive thoughts, often repetitive and at times perhaps even debilitating—are not particularly exceptional cases, but rather a phenomenon much closer to a norm. What is at stake here is the father's confrontation with whatever he most fears may befall his child, and usually what he most fears for his child has some significant autobiographical grounding. What is at stake is the father's coming to terms with the possibility of the defacement of his child's innocence and purity. I spoke early on in these pages about the kinds of traumas that the parent most fears. We may be speaking of a severe illness, various forms of abuse, social traumas related to the school environment (e.g., bullying), or any other of a great variety of traumas the child may undergo, extending all the way even to the death of the child.

To face the unthinkable thought without any means of escape is to stand passive before the possibility of the evential blow reaching my child and thus fundamentally reshaping them. It is a feeling of helplessness in the face of terror. There is within the father who absorbs this evential blow a courage to sit still in the terror's "sunken place," to "take it," as it were, to accept that there is in this moment no escape. Here he faces that which he perhaps never thought he would have to face, that which he certainly never wished to face, to accept the possibility of the unthinkable, to accept that the unthinkable does sometimes happen, and can he accept that this possibility may indeed come to pass, can he advene himself to the risks his child faces? As the father faces the unthinkable, he finds his fortitude tested by the acids of terror. Should this unthinkable trauma come to pass for his child, will the father be able to accommodate himself to this new reality the event has cast for the child, will he be able to accept the need for his child to advene from their pre-event self to their post-event self, all their possibilities now shaken and re-thrown by the traumatic event? Without any means of escape, the father must in this moment face the thought of the unthinkable, must learn to dwell under the terror of the unthinkable and yet trust, to exist without shield, totally exposed to the unthinkable thoughts that sometimes terrorize him, accepting their possibility, that the child may indeed undergo in their life the trauma of the unthinkable. Romano describes well this kind of responsibility of exposure:

> To be able to hold open the opening of his possibility by holding himself there, to have the capacity to persist in this openness, through which an advenant is exposed to more than he is capable of—this is what I call "responsibility." I can answer for myself and be "responsible" only if I can first answer *to* an event in its impersonal occurring, only if I can face what happens to me [or in our case, to my child]. It is solely on this condition that I can also be responsible *for* an event—that in itself cannot be taken over—that is, I can hold myself free *for* it, open and available, by submitting myself to a transformation. . . . To be oneself is to persist in this openness of measureless exposure to events, to set oneself free for them, to be *available*. Responsibility is strictly this empty space of pure availability to what happens to us.[9]

For the father to accept such psychic conditions, to hold oneself open to the unthinkable thought, to the possibility of his child's trauma, is itself a kind of sacrifice borne for the love of his child, this inability to think away the unthinkable, to love in its midst, to savor his child to the limits of savoring, all the way to (the thought of) the utmost sacrifice, a sacrifice more torturous than substitution, the inability to substitute himself and undergo the trauma in his child's place, a substitution that he would undertake in an instant with no hesitations whatsoever, were such a substitution possible. Neurotic though it may be, this is nothing other than love at its limits, the place where the father's existential exposure, his own utmost vulnerability, meets that of his child, unarmored before the violence the traumatic event may inflict.

As it turns out, one of the greatest acts of love the father can undertake is to bring his own vulnerability as an offering to his child, to love

9. Romano, *Event and World*, 94–95.

his child to the point where his finitude sets the firmest limits and where he finds himself powerless to save his child but nonetheless compelled to show up for them, to stay with them. The father's highest responsibility is this surrender at the limits, this willingness to be exposed to the elements together with his child. This is the place where responsibility becomes prayer, and prayer becomes responsibility, this stepping out into the elements for the child's sake in a manner of faith and trust, this surrender out in the weather, come what may, light or dark, warm or cold.

Conclusion

THERE ARE OF COURSE both risks and rewards to thinking extensively about the early years of the father–child relation while still immersed in the experience of those early years of raising a young child. As I write this conclusion, my daughter is now four years old, and in the last few months we have just welcomed her baby sister as well. The foremost benefit of this arrangement for relating my life and my thinking has been the immediacy of the phenomena. I am jotting down the experiences right after undergoing them, and so there is much less distance between the event and the thinking and writing, and therefore less blunting of the force with which the phenomena have arrived. Everything is right there in front of me, or at least can be called up fairly easily from recent memory. I can readily recall my daughter's emergence from the womb, her bluish-purple face, her motionless body resting in the bassinet, the resuscitator taped to her mouth. It was not so long ago, after all, so when I recall this, at least if I let myself linger in that memory, all the panic and importance of the moment washes over me again. All the phenomena are fresh enough that I am able to some extent to re-enter my experience of them without too much difficulty, to remember the experiential textures and savors of the events that have passed in these early years of my daughter's life.

But I also wonder whether, in five or ten years' time, I will look back on this book and think that my description was too myopic. I cannot predict the future, of course, but I will be curious to see if in due time the experiences I have described here will feel like one small but important part of my relationship with my daughter. My sense of her personhood and my understanding of the influence I have had on her as a father will surely change over time. Perhaps I will even come to think that I was a bit melodramatic in those early years, taken aback as I was by the unrelenting evential force of my daughter's first few years on this earth. Caught up in the dense miasma that is family life, and especially those early years

53

of family life, I do not have the distance to see through the fog. I have no clear view up on a hilltop, up away at a remove from all the details of my life with my family, no spot from which I can look on and observe it all without always already being intimately involved. Therefore, there is really no way for me to place the phenomena I experience as a father on any kind of a map of the terrain that would give me a sense for what lies outside the areas I have explored. Perhaps I can do this intellectually. I can think about my daughter as a teenager or as a young woman. I can think about how the view might look significantly different later on. This might even help me to see my daughter in the light of a much longer story that comprises her full life. Such thoughts might even give me a sense of pace in my fatherhood, of the need for patience and for surrender. All this is well and good. Indeed, probably all parents should undertake such mental exercises as a way of seeing their child's life in a larger frame. But still the fact remains that these phenomena that are futural in orientation can only ever operate on the plane of the imagination, never in the reality that meets me today. They are never more than mental phenomena that, though certainly of great importance, cannot account for the phenomenal fullness of the now, even in all the slippage of the present moment. Though the now slips away and floats on downstream into the past, it is only ever the present and the past that are real and that therefore carry a certain phenomenal fullness that the future by its nature can never offer.

Then again, it may also be that time has a way, if we are not spiritually discerning and deliberate, of dulling our sense of the existential heft we meet in the face of another human person, even when that person is a dearly loved one, even when that person was once a young child who, in her most vulnerable moments, looked at me with tear-soaked eyes and quivering lips, her face wrenched with some new pain. I am speaking of the past now. The most mature father knows that it does him no good to look back at the past and wish he had been more prepared. If he is attentive to his experience of time, he will know that as a finite creature he was and is constitutively incapable of preparing for the present moments that are now passed, always passing, always passed. This is precisely what I have meant when I have spoken of the evential violences of time. It is in the nature of human experience that we are always late to the moment, inadequately meeting it, unsure where it came from or how it moved past us so quickly. In such a setting, awash in the finitude we as parents share with our children, the only proper response can be attention and wonder, and a steady, patient vigilance, an openness, an exposure even, as we continue allowing ourselves to be affected by our children, to have our attention captivated and our hearts and minds awestruck by the excess we meet in their faces. Our children, soul-full creatures that they are, deserve nothing less. Certainly my two daughters, whose beautiful brown eyes never cease calling for their father's love, deserve nothing less.

Bibliography

Bugbee, Henry. *The Inward Morning: A Philosophical Exploration in Journal Form.* Athens, GA: The University of Georgia Press, 1999.

Carnes, Natalie. *Motherhood: A Confession.* Stanford: Stanford University Press, 2020.

Cavanaugh, William T. *Being Consumed: Economics and Christian Desire.* Grand Rapids: Eerdmans, 2008.

Chrétien, Jean-Louis. *The Call and the Response.* Translated by Anne A. Davenport. New York: Fordham University Press, 2004.

———. *Ten Meditations for Catching and Losing One's Breath.* Translated by Steven DeLay. Kalos. Eugene, OR: Cascade, 2024.

DeLay, Steven. *Phenomenology in France: A Philosophical and Theological Introduction.* London: Routledge, 2019.

Falque, Emmanuel. *Crossing the Rubicon: The Borderlands of Philosophy and Theology.* Translated by Reuben Shank. Perspectives in Continental Philosophy. New York: Fordham University Press, 2016.

Francis, Pope. *Amoris Laetitia.* https://www.vatican.va/content/dam/francesco/pdf/apost_exhortations/documents/papa-francesco_esortazione-ap_20160319_amoris-laetitia_en.pdf.

Han, Byung-Chul. *The Burnout Society.* Translated by Erik Butler. Stanford Briefs. Stanford: Stanford University Press, 2015.

———. *In the Swarm: Digital Prospects.* Translated by Erik Butler. Untimely Meditations. Cambridge: The MIT Press, 2017.

———. *The Scent of Time: A Philosophical Essay on the Art of Lingering.* Translated by Daniel Steuer. Medford, MA: Polity, 2017.

Henry, Michel. *Incarnation: A Philosophy of Flesh.* Translated by Karl Hefty. Northwestern University Studies in Phenomenology and Existential Philosophy. Evanston, IL: Northwestern University Press, 2015.

Knausgaard, Karl Ove. *Autumn.* Translated by Ingvild Burkey. New York: Penguin, 2017.

Lacoste, Jean-Yves. *Experience and the Absolute: Disputed Questions on the Humanity of Man.* Translated by Mark Raftery. Perspectives in Continental Philosophy. New York: Fordham University Press, 2004.

———. *From Theology to Theological Thinking.* Translated by W. Chris Hackett. Charlottesville, VA: University of Virginia Press, 2014.

Levinas, Emmanuel. *Otherwise Than Being, or, Beyond Essence.* Translated by Alphonso Lingis. Pittsburgh: Duquesne University Press, 1998.

————. *Totality and Infinity: An Essay on Exteriority*. Translated by Alphonso Lingis. Pittsburgh, PA: Duquesne University Press, 1969.

Lewis, C. S. *The Weight of Glory and Other Addresses*. New York: HarperOne, 2001.

Marion, Jean-Luc. *In Excess: Studies of Saturated Phenomena*. Translated by Robyn Horner and Vincent Berraud. Perspectives in Continental Philosophy. New York: Fordham University Press, 2004.

Mickel, Zechariah. "Luminaries / John Milbank / Metaphysics and Radical(ized) Orthodoxy." *The Theology Mill* podcast, October 31, 2023. https://wipfandstock. com/blog/2023/10/31/luminaries-john-milbank-metaphysics-and-radicalized-orthodoxy/.

Pietersma, Henry. *Phenomenological Epistemology*. New York: Oxford University Press, 2000.

Rivera, Joseph. *Phenomenology and the Horizon of Experience: Spiritual Themes in Henry, Marion, and Lacoste*. Routledge New Critical Thinking in Religion, Theology and Biblical Studies. London: Routledge, 2022.

Robbins, Jill, ed. *Is It Righteous to Be? Interviews with Emmanuel Levinas*. Meridian: Crossing Aesthetics. Stanford: Stanford University Press, 2001.

Romano, Claude. *Event and World*. Translated by Shane Mackinlay. Perspectives in Continental Philosophy. New York: Fordham University Press, 2009.

Rosa, Hartmut. *Social Acceleration: A New Theory of Modernity*. New Directions in Critical Theory. New York: Columbia University Press, 2015.

Wallenfang, Donald. *Phenomenology: A Basic Introduction in the Light of Jesus Christ*. Cascade Companions. Eugene, OR: Cascade, 2019.

Index

www.ingramcontent.com/pod-product-compliance
Lightning Source LLC
Chambersburg PA
CBHW022038090426
42741CB00007B/1117